ST. FRANCIS OF ASSISI

BY T.S.R. BOASE
LITHOGRAPHS BY ARTHUR BOYD

In all of history, few men have experimented more sincerely with the literal practice of the teachings of Jesus than Francesco Bernadone of Assisi. Because of this, his life has had an arresting quality on men of different eras and philosophies. Franciscan history has become a field of research in itself and has been the lifelong vocation of many scholars. The first *Life of St. Francis* was written by Thomas of Celano, who had joined the Order in 1215. Since Celano's biography, numerous books have attempted to capture the fearless sincerity, poetry of action, and charm that characterized St. Francis. Although this charm has remained undefined and no two of his friends or biographers have agreed on exactly where it lay, it continues to draw men to him nearly eight centuries after his death. St. Francis is not an easy subject for exacting measurement and explanation; each man will develop his own interpretation. In this biography, which has been thoroughly revised to include the findings of current research in Franciscan history, Mr. Boase presents the general outlines of the many facets of St. Francis' life, carefully placing St. Francis in relation to the historical, social, and philosophical movements of the thirteenth century. In a set of lithographs prepared especially for this book, Mr. Arthur Boyd has reinterpreted the Franciscan legend in twentieth-century terms.

T. S. R. BOASE, President of Magdelen College, Oxford University, is editor of the *Oxford History of English Art* to which he has contributed two volumes, *English Art 1100–1216* and *English Art 1800–1870*. He is author of CHRIST BEARING THE CROSS : *Attributed to Valdes Leal.*

ARTHUR BOYD is internationally acclaimed as one of Australia's finest and most original artists. His paintings have won high praise at exhibitions in Melbourne and London, and he is equally well known for his outstanding work in sculpture, stage design, ceramics, and lithography.

ST FRANCIS OF ASSISI

ST. FRANCIS OF ASSISI

T. S. R. BOASE

with 16 lithographs by

ARTHUR BOYD

INDIANA UNIVERSITY PRESS
BLOOMINGTON AND LONDON

FIRST PUBLISHED IN THE UNITED STATES 1968
ALL RIGHTS RESERVED
COPYRIGHT © 1968 BY THAMES AND HUDSON, LONDON
LIBRARY OF CONGRESS CATALOG CARD NUMBER: 68–15550
PRINTED IN GREAT BRITAIN

CONTENTS

LIST OF ILLUSTRATIONS

PREFACE

THIS brief life of St Francis was first published thirty years ago in 1936. Re-reading it, I have, not surprisingly, found here and there phrases that no longer exactly express my opinions. The language of Christian conviction has been changing, and much of the old symbolism that then could be used confidently, with its traditional beauties still valid, has gradually become unserviceable for modern concepts. I have changed some passages and altered here and there the emphasis, but it is still the same book and St Francis still means the same to me as when I first wrote it.

Factual correction is an easier matter. Research on Franciscan history has continued and Dr Moorman in his sources for the Life of St Francis (1940) reopened many problems. I have made some modifications, but in a work of this scale there is no possibility of investigating points of detail, and here too the main outlines are the same.

The pictures that illustrate it are completely new, essentially of the 1960s, and the re-printing of this book is largely to provide a background for them. Within a few years of his death, there were paintings of St Francis. In the Sacro Speco at Subiaco there is a wall-painting of *Frater Franciscus,* where the absence of a halo strongly suggests that the painting must precede his canonization on 16 July 1228. The features are simply but convincingly drawn, and the large eyes light up the thin, bearded face. In his hand he

holds a scroll with his familiar greeting 'Pax huic domini'. That
it is a likeness is perhaps too much to expect, but for all its naïveté it
is a very satisfactory suggestion of the man.

In 1235 Bonaventura Berlinghieri painted and signed an altarpiece in the church of San Francesco at Pescia. Here Francis has
become a haloed saint, displaying the marks of the stigmata and
surrounded by small scenes from his legend, the vision on Monte
La Verna, the preaching to the birds, the healing of Bartolomeo
da Narni, and three miracles at his tomb. It is an object of cult, an
invocation to a miracle worker. There are other such paintings from
the thirteenth century, but it is, fittingly, in the upper church at
Assisi that the legend takes its memorable visual form. Who was
the designer of the series, on which several hands were at work,
remains a question of recurrent and at the moment almost inter-
national debate. Vasari, visiting Assisi in 1563, accepted the tradition that the Franciscan frescoes in the Upper Church were by
Giotto, but that is a statement two hundred and fifty years after
the event, and, though there is early record of Giotto working in
Assisi, it is not till the sixteenth century that the Franciscan scenes
are definitely assigned to him. Certainly others, such as the Master of
St Cecilia or Marino da Perugia, are candidates for a considerable
participation. If not by Giotto, the paintings have Giottesque
elements, and his name will always be associated with them. They
were the first great rendering in Italian art of a new theme, and they
were to have many followers, very notably in the mid-quattrocento
the frescoes of Benozzo Gozzoli at Montefalco and the altarpiece
painted by Sassetta for the church of San Francesco in Borgo San
Sepolcro.

The legend, with its mingling of fact and fable, has remained a
pictorial inspiration. The ordinariness of St Francis, that he himself
always stressed, and his imaginative perception of things spiritual
have formed a great myth of the meeting of everyday life and the
hints and guesses that lie beyond it, the frontier between observation
and vision. Van Eyck, Bellini, Rubens – the list could be a long one.
And now today artists with a very different background and outlook,

but with the conviction that 'in the growth and transformation of its myths a society achieves its own sense of identity',[1] have turned again to St Francis. Sidney Nolan has shewn the floating, crucified Christ appearing to the saint against a wide background of hills that is half the Maremma and half the outback. Now Arthur Boyd, leaving the Australian myth of the Half-caste Bride, is using his large, passionate grotesque figures, huge descendants of Hieronymus Bosch, to re-translate the old story into twentieth-century terms. The terms in which he re-creates the legend are very different from the idealism of the quattrocento. These huge, shining faces, these squat, often insistently nude creatures, have an earthy, brutal quality that is in many ways nearer the facts than the older versions, evocative as these were of the Umbrian setting; and tenderness is not lacking, particularly in the scenes with St Clare, a subject that has stirred Boyd so deeply. And where, as in the meeting of St Francis and the Wolf, the figures blend into one another or are absorbed into the setting, this is contemporary parlance, rightly applied to a still valid theme.

1. *The Antipodean Manifesto,* preface to the Antipodean Exibition held in Melbourne in 1959. The Manifesto is a statement of the continuing need of figurative as opposed to abstract art. Arthur Boyd was one of the signatories.

PLATE I

ST FRANCIS AND THE REVELS IN ASSISI

'*So vain and bizarre was he that sometimes on the same garment he would sew patches of worthless cloth beside pieces of the richest material.*' *As a young man leading the revels in Assisi, he was 'on a sudden visited by the Lord, and his heart was filled with such sweetness that he could not speak . . . And his companions asked him "what are you thinking of; why do you not come with us. Perhaps you are thinking of taking a wife". To whom he replied "You speak true, a bride nobler and richer and fairer than you have ever seen". And they derided him. But thus he said not of himself but of God, for his bride was true religion.' (Legenda Trium Sociorum CC.I and III)*

St Francis, in his patchwork cloak, turns away from two lovers, wrapt in his own meditations.

15—25

CHAPTER ONE

THERE are in the teaching of Christ as handed down in the Gospels certain hard sayings: 'Take no thought for the morrow ... Go and sell that thou hast, and give to the poor ... Turn the other cheek also ... He who would save his life must lose it' – words that are often taken as said in particular contexts with particular and limited applications, but which can still perturb the individual conscience. It is because, in the records of history, few men have experimented more honestly in the literal practice of these sayings than Francesco Bernardone of Assisi, that his life-story has had such an arresting quality for men of very varied periods and temperaments.

He had not only fearless sincerity, but also a persuasive personality, a poetry of action that attracted all who met him; and though this charm could not be defined, and no two of his friends could quite agree wherein it lay, yet it lives after him and continues its spell. Today, all who know anything of St Francis know that he was lovable. That is certain, among all the varying accounts of his life's incidents, and if some of these seem harsh and foolish, we are prepared to interpret them with an affectionate tolerance, until we learn enough from them to know that tolerance towards St Francis can only be a kind of arrogance.

Even before he died there were among his followers divergent views as to the aim of the Order that he had created, and the

beginnings of bitterness and hostility. The disputes centred on the
interpretation of the rule, but they inevitably involved differing
emphases on the character and actions of the founder. The first
Life of St Francis was written, probably between 1229 and 1231, by
Thomas of Celano, who had joined the Order in 1215, had
played a prominent part in the missions to Germany, and had it
seems been with St Francis in the last two years of his life; not one of
the most intimate circle, but a respected and reliable witness. The
early years of Francis are sketchily dealt with, and little attempt seems
to have been made to secure information about them. There is little
said about the dissensions within the Order, though, unlike the
background of Assisi, they must have been well known to Celano.
Miracle stories, possibly collected for the canonization in 1228, bulk
large. The problem of Celano's other sources has been a matter of
much controversy. There are various works, dating in the form in
which they have come down to us from the early fourteenth century,
which undoubtedly include reminiscences set down by Francis's
closest friends. One of these books, known as the *Legend of the
Three Companions,* contains material that was used by Celano. The
Legend however has an introductory letter stating that it was compiled
in 1246 by Leo, Angelo and Rufino, who were with Francis
throughout many of the crises of his career. This letter must refer to a
later stage, when Celano was revising his work for a *Second Life,* a
revision asked for by the General Chapter of 1244, which also
invited all those who had known the saint to send in writing their
memories of him. The introductory letter must have been a reply to
this request, though it is now attached to earlier material that
Celano had already used. It is possible also that Leo in 1246
repeated information he had previously supplied. What is certain is
that much first-hand material was deposited at Assisi, some of which,
given the disputes in the Order, must have been inflammatory
stuff. The views of the intimate friends, 'we who were with him',
retained the intransigence they had learned from their founder. In
1260 it was ordered that all earlier writings should be withdrawn,
and yet another *Life* written by the Minister General, Bonaventura.

It is this *Life,* based largely on those of Celano, that has represented Francis throughout the greater part of the time that separates us from him. It is a noble and dignified book infused with genuine fervour, but it is a work of edification. Bonaventura was a trained and subtle theologian, a mystic with the technique of visions. His Francis remains a figure of great vitality and charm, but a little straitened in a particular convention. To the devout Catholic mind it was in keeping with accepted theories of sanctity, and, as such, satisfactory: and, with much other noble literature, the Protestant countries of Europe, after the Reformation, left it on one side, and for a time St Francis was little thought of. But not wholly forgotten. His story remained familiar because of its pictorial qualities. When in the nineteenth century the paintings of the Italian primitives came back into favour, the Franciscan legend was remembered with them, and the tales of him written in Italian in the fourteenth century, *I Fioretti del glorioso messere San Francesco e de' suoi Frati,* were translated and in much demand in northern Europe. Of all the saints of the Catholic Church, Francis has most freely transcended religious divisions. Two great thinkers of the mid-century, Renan and Ruskin, proclaimed their admiration for the Poverello, and Renan's insight and penetration revealed in Francis qualities which conventionally pious biographies obscured: it was, moreover, his writings which inspired one of his pupils, Paul Sabatier, to devote himself to the study of the Franciscan sources and to bring out in 1894 the first edition of his *Vie de St François.* Born in 1858, son of a Protestant pastor in the Cevennes, himself in orders, Sabatier found time to write only after political sympathies had banished him from a parish in Strasbourg, ill health from a curacy in his native mountains. His approach to St Francis was that of a Protestant, bred in that most uncompromising Protestantism of southern France, and of a liberal taught by the great freethinker Renan: the life of a medieval saint would hardly have appeared a congenial task. But in the history of the cult of St Francis his book is a landmark, in that it went back behind the tradition of the Church, behind Bonaventura's stylistic masterpiece, to portray the saint as he had appeared to those who knew him. Sabatier's dating of some of the material he used cannot be maintained in face of later research. He thought that one work, the *Mirror of Perfection,* was written by Leo as early as 1227, when it is in fact one of the fourteenth-century compilations, based on these documents deposited at Assisi in the 1240s. Despite the withdrawal of all other accounts ordered when Bonaventura's *Life* was written, some of this deposit of contemporary accounts must have remained, at least for a time, in the Assisian archives, and selections from it passed into circulation amongst the Spirituals, the upholders of the original Rule. It is little wonder that Sabatier made some errors in this almost uncharted and bewildering field of Franciscan historiography, but he had a sympathetic insight that led him very unfailingly to the significant and genuinely early passages in the material he was using. His St Francis is the Francis of Brother Leo, of the companions who 'were with him' – men who resented much that was happening in the Order in the closing years of Francis's life, who wrote with a certain prejudice, but who wrote lovingly of one whom they knew well as a living man, not as a saint raised upon the altars. And their picture of him conquered Sabatier: underneath the medieval asceticism, the piety of another age, he saw a burning Christian spirit, akin to all that was noblest in his own beliefs. In himself he was well qualified for his under-taking. Again, as with Bonaventura, a man had been found worthy to interpret saints. The *Vie de St François,* now in its forty-seventh edition, was translated into almost every European language. It was a rediscovery. Since then Franciscan history has become a field of research in itself, the life-work of many scholars – *franciscanisants* the French call them – the subject of many specialized periodicals, and, in the world at large, a new inspiration to Catholics and Protestants alike.

The life of St Francis is not a subject for exact measurement and explanation: every man will find his own interpretation of it, seeing by its light some reproach to his own ways; for those who find in it no quality of illumination will hardly understand it, and, if they trouble to read of him, must be content to wonder only. It is the reproach that matters: given that, textual criticism, psychological or physiological speculation (and there has been plenty of both) are lesser things. We today have to learn new adaptations of religious terminology, but this fearless exponent of basic interpretations can still communicate with us despite the medievalism of his setting.

Assisi on its hillside beyond the Tiber valley – the early Tiber, a small yellow stream with frequent tributaries – has changed little; the fortress above still merges with the stony hilltop, and if newer houses have backed against the old walls, and, newest of all, some villas have straggled towards the railway station in the plain, yet the town keeps its site, with the rugged, small duomo in the centre, which Francis saw clean cut and white and just completed; only now the outline of buildings ends in the tower and colonnade of San Francesco, its most memorable familiar feature, and below there is the large, assertive dome of Sta Maria degli Angeli, encasing the minute Porziuncola, the early Franciscan home. Assisi has become the place of pilgrimage, the town of Il Santo; it has its hotels, its consciousness of the past, its odd corners of tiresome tourist piety. In 1181/2, when Francis was born, the townspeople looked forward, thinking little of what had gone before. The wars of pope and emperor which passed up and down Umbria were for them a means of obtaining more and more civic freedom – freedom for self-government and for angry minor wars among themselves; freedom, too, for their expanding trade, which brought new contacts with France and other lands beyond the mountains. At the turn of the century Assisi made a great gesture of independence. For some twenty years they had been under imperial control, ruled, not too exactingly, by the German Conrad, Duke of Spoleto – 'Old Nit-Wit' they called him, with that love of nicknames in which Francis shared. But in 1197 the Emperor Henry VI died suddenly and immaturely, leaving his young son Frederick a helpless child. In the confusion that followed, Pope Innocent III sought to regain control of papal territory, and Duke Conrad, finding himself unsupported, gave up his lands to Rome. His favourite residence of late had been the Rocca, the castle of Assisi; and the citizens

celebrated his departure by pulling it down and using its stones to
build walls round their city. On a stone of the archway can still be
read the date – 'This work was done in the year of our Lord, 1199'
– and, underneath, the name of the city's leader: 'Under the con-
sulship of Tancred.' For, like many another commune in Italy,
Assisi was seeking to protect her liberty by institutions as well as
fortifications, and, freed from the imperial legate, she had elected
from her citizens consuls to direct her affairs. Innocent III might
protest that Assisi had returned to papal rule, not found an unheard-of liberty; but the citizens remained firm, continuing their
wall building, and Innocent had larger affairs to busy him.

The new wall, however, protected only their houses; outside
were the lands of the commune, and, overlooking them from the
crags and spurs of Monte Subasio, the castles of the nobles, Sassorosso, Montenoro, Poggio San Damiano, and such-like; from these
fastnesses the lords exacted heavy tolls on the citizens' trade, and
sought to hold them within the old framework of feudal services,
demanding the fulfilment of ancient customs which often, no
doubt, ran counter to more recent labour requirements in the city.
Here, as elsewhere in Italy, the struggle was beginning between
power based on land and power based on merchandise, and policies
of trade were transcending the local interests in which petty lordships
had first consideration. The death of Henry, the slackening of
imperial prestige, weakened the feudal position; not only the Rocca
fell, but other castles also, and the communal militia, in this
moment of triumph, left only fragments of them, impossible to
rebuild. Then wider disputes were revived by this civil broil of
burghers and nobles; the three sons of Gislerio, lord of Sassorosso,
with other Assisian nobles, called on Perugia for assistance, and
finally the two towns warred together. Each sought the help of
neighbours from the surrounding hill country: Foligno, allied with
Perugia, threatened Assisi from the south-east, but the smaller
townships allied themselves under the red and blue flag which
Assisi carried to battle – Nocera, Bevagna, Spello, Rosciano,
Bastia, all names soon to have their sacred memories. From the city

itself, all from eighteen to sixty years of age served in the army; and
amongst them Francis Bernardone, son of a wealthy merchant,
being well able to afford the expense involved, provided his horse
and equipment and fought with the cavalry. 'He was of knightly
manners,' writes one of his early biographers, but the knightliness
in the matter of fighting rank had a sound cash basis, and was itself
part of the invasion of feudalism by the merchants, who claimed
old privileges by new pretensions. The little armies, for their levies
came in tens and twenties, met in the valley between their towns,
at Collestrada, where a bridge across the Tiber holds the approach
to Perugia. The battle was fought with all the violence of their
'antique hate'.

> Fallen are the Lords of Assisi, and their limbs are all mangled,
> Torn apart and defaced, so their own cannot know them;
> There is no head where the foot is, the entrails are scattered,
> The eye no longer looks from the socket, its one-time window.

So, in rude Latin, wrote a Perugian poet, celebrating his citizens'
victory and savagery. The Assisians were routed, many slain,
many of their costly horses killed or captured, many prisoners
taken, amongst them Francis, who doubtless suffered the usual
indignities, for it was customary in Perugia to march their prisoners
bound through the streets, dragging their conquered banners in
the dirt behind them; and though he was lodged with the nobles,
having fought amongst them, it was probably a hard and miserable
enough confinement; from which after a year or so he was released, it
seems on grounds of sickness. There was in Perugia a guild for
tending sick prisoners and aiding their ransom and return, a curious
softening of the brutality of the times.

Assisi, though defeated, had not been crushed. At the opening of
the year (1203) they in turn had some successes in the field; and that
autumn, to strengthen their hands against Perugia, they offered
amends to the feudal nobility. All those who had left the city
'from the time that the commune had war with Perugia' were
declared banished and their lands forfeited; those, however, who

had proved loyal were to receive houses in the town, built for them at the commune's expense, and the old feudal services were to be rendered to them, unless a long prescriptive right – twenty-four years – had established their lapse. It is an instructive document. The merchant citizens, the *popolo grosso,* have brought the nobles within the city's circuit, where they can watch their doings and have the advantage of their military aid; the independence of their country castles is forbidden them, but, in compensation, the commune pays for their new palaces, and their old rights over the peasants, the *popolo minuto,* are restored to them, for the peasant or the humble weaver or the carrier or scavenger in the town has no voice strong enough to make his claim heard.

Perugia was not the only enemy to be feared: since papal protest against the destruction of the Rocca, Assisi had been suspicious of Innocent's patrimonial policy, his desire for new authority over the Umbrian cities, his known friendship for Perugia. Bishop Guido of Assisi, an intriguing, not over-popular man, had had reason to complain that his excommunications were neglected; in defiance of papal authority the citizens re-elected as consul Girardo dei Gilberti, who had led them at Collestrada, but now lay under excommuni-cation. Innocent placed Assisi for a time under interdict, until the city came to terms. And all the time, as the public notary wearily marked on the margin of a document, 'there was war between

PLATE II

ST FRANCIS DREAMING OF A HUNCHBACK

'When the enemy of the human race perceived this good commencement he strove to draw him back from it. Now there was a certain woman in Assisi deformed with a hunched back, whom the demon kept bringing to the mind of the man of God, threatening him that the hunchback of this woman would fall on him, unless he forsook the work he had undertaken.' (Legenda Trium Sociorum C.IV)

15—25

Perugia and Assisi' – war at close quarters, of constant skirmishes. Nocera, captured by Perugia, was regained by Assisi; but money failed, and neither side could hire more soldiers; in the summer of 1205 the two rival towns began to treat, each bargaining on behalf of the other's disloyal exiles. In such a world of dispute and intrigue lived the young Francis, a member of that merchant class whose rise to power was the revolutionary and disturbing force – a hard world, as the world is at all crises of transition. In the grants made by pious Assisians to their Cathedral in these years of war and accompanying famine comes again and again the refrain, not merely formally, 'Since the life of man is brief and blind and full of many miseries and various tribulations.'

His father, Peter Bernardone, dealt in woollen cloth 'of diverse colours' such as was better woven in Italy than elsewhere. When his wife, Pica, bore her first son, he was as far afield as France, and the boy had been baptized John before his return; but, because of his journey, he called him Francis – or so, afterwards, it was said – and Francis always seemed to hold France in special affection. There is no record that as a boy he ever went there with his father, but none the less its influence was strong. He learned to speak its language, doubtless from traders visiting his father, and in the wool business some French was a necessary asset. But to Francis it stood for tales of romance and troubadour songs – it was in his happy moments that he used it, making his jests and catchwords and sometimes his songs in it, and begging often in French as though to purify this language of the counting-house. It was in southern France that the best songs were sung, and it was from across the hills that Francis learned of Charlemagne and Arthur and was seized with delight in the Gothic chivalry of the knightly life. But along this same channel came other ideas, less spoken of by Francis, less directly marked in his conversation, but of undoubted influence upon him, and added reasons why his thoughts at some times formed themselves in French.

For France was the land of heresies. Already at Rome Innocent was coming to the conviction that only extermination could save

Europe from the dangerous teachings spreading from Languedoc. In that early ripened culture there had been a desire for new freedoms, and old Eastern beliefs, which set spirit and body in contrast and denied the Christian fusion, found there a strange receptivity; on the one side were the enthusiasms and ascetic fire of the elect, on the other a carefree licence, counting on the indifference of fleshly acts. It had its attractions; it was a clear statement, an easy essay in black and white. Where the Church was unpopular, where the local bishop or priest was conspicuously lacking in Christian virtues – and such cases were not rare, where some monastery had fallen from its early strictness, there the exalted confessors of this dubious faith found converts. The doctrine of the Incarnation, that the Word became flesh, was made to seem a compromise, rather than the only solution. Down into Italy the teaching penetrated; close to Assisi, at Viterbo and Orvieto, there were strong demonstrations of it. Francis was acquainted with the idea of heresy, and this was one form in which he knew it. But there were heresies of another kind; men who had been forced into heresy almost against their will, in particular the followers of Peter Waldo, the Poor Men of Lyons. In the new industrial centres, in Lyons, in Milan, the hand-workers, weavers and so forth, were finding a new prosperity, and finding, also, little place for themselves in the existing feudal scheme of society. The Church thought feudally about its income, and in too many cases somewhat feudally about the souls in its charge. In rare instances only had it anything to give to men prepared to stand on a position of new independence, men like these Waldensians, who already wished to read the Bible in their own vernacular tongue. Receiving little nourishment from the Church, they started preaching on their own, not questioning doctrine, but attacking a Church too occupied with the affairs of this world to attend to other-worldly business. To begin with, the papacy welcomed them; but, as bishops grew restless under this local criticism, the popes also turned against them; preaching was forbidden them, and the Poor Men of Lyons, refusing to abandon their evangelizing, found themselves cast out. Such had been the situation when Innocent III came to the papal chair, with clearer wisdom than his predecessors. Prepared in Languedoc to stamp out heresy by force, he was, amongst these vaguer, pious movements, anxious above all to guide them, to secure their enthusiasms for the Church's service, to use their criticism as a stimulus or to dull its edge by recognition of its claims. In Lombardy there were Poor Men of Milan, Humiliati, they called themselves, weavers mainly, pooling their resources, and living together a common life of prayer and industry, by which they found for themselves some place in a difficult world and in which both men and women joined. Innocent, in 1201, made a Rule for them, giving them protection, allowing them even some rights of preaching.

Such ideas, coming down the trade routes, were the daily news of an Assisian merchant and very familiar thoughts to the young Francis.

CHAPTER TWO

FRANCIS had come to Assisi, from his Perugian captivity, sick and with bitter memories. Years afterwards his followers still noted how his voice shook 'complainingly' when he spoke of 'the much wrong that the men of Perugia did to those of Assisi'. But at the time he was not long downcast. Cheerfulness and self-confidence are the general burden of the early stories of him. 'I shall be a great man,' he told his companions in prison – in no strict prophetic sense, for his hopes then were on feats of arms and knightly conduct. His first experience of warfare might have been discouraging, but within two years he was keenly bent on another expedition. Count Gentile da Fabriano, who had come to Assisi's aid but found his promised pay not forthcoming was departing for new wars in Apulia. Francis 'aspired to go with him and be knighted by him'. There were great preparations, for Francis was known for his splendid attire, and had in dress the exuberance and fastidiousness of a young man trying his paces, of the merchant lad, who had set the fashion for the young aristocrats: he had had a cloak that was much talked of, a patchwork of rich pieces and old rags. So the armour and robes prepared were 'planned with all liberality, ingenious and costly'; and Francis dreamed at night of spears and glittering shields and other accoutrements. 'I know,' he kept saying, 'that I shall be a great man.' But at the last moment his exit from Assisi was not so magnificent as had been planned, for he found a penniless knight, one of the city's unpaid mercenaries, unable to equip himself, and gave most of his own equipment to him. It was an impulse of courtesy, not done without effort. When Leo tells the story, which he must have heard from Francis himself, the splendid armour is an exciting matter, not easily parted with. It was made thoughtful by a real act of sacrifice that Francis left Assisi. They spent the first night at Spoleto – a sleepless night for Francis, for it was in it that he determined that the knightly life of arms was not that to which he was called; that the arms he had dreamt of were not earthly arms, and his Lord no mere local count; that he had not known, in Bonaventura's experienced phrase, 'to pass through the appearance of things seen to the behold⁄ing of things unseen.' He returned to Assisi and abandoned the expedition to the south.

His conversion was, however, no sudden one. Francis was not of those, such as Paul or Augustine, who find in some supernatural event the cataclysmic realization of a change of heart. Francis seems to have come to it rather by growing thoughtfulness. His early heed⁄less extravagances had been open⁄handed, and his peculiar attraction had come from liveliness combined with purity of mind. One of his biographers, it is true, Thomas of Celano, tries to heighten the

PLATE III

ST FRANCIS KISSES THE HAND OF A LEPER

'*When he was riding near Assisi, he met a leper on his path. And since he had been wont to have much horror of lepers, doing violence on himself, he dismounted, and offered him alms, kissing his hand. And having received the kiss of peace from him, he remounted and proceeded on his way. And so he began more and more to humble himself until by the grace of God he reached fully victory over himself.*' (*Legenda Trium Sociorum C.IV*)

15—25

effect by describing a youthful career of wantonness, but to do so he has to echo phrases from Augustine's *Confessions,* and the picture is a clearly conventional one. 'He was,' says Leo, on the other hand, 'of a natural courtesy in word and deed after the prompting of his heart.' And Bonaventura endorses that view: 'He went not astray after the lust of the flesh, albeit given up unto pleasures.' On his return from Spoleto there was no immediate change of ways; only, when he led revels through Assisi, he would grow thoughtful, so that they laughed and said he was in love, and he answered: 'Yes, with one fairer than any they had seen.' For he was already thinking of Lady Poverty. *(Pl. I)*

So he began to draw apart, talking much with one particular friend whose name none of the chroniclers give us; nor do we know exactly what were the discussions between them, though it is not hard to see something of the problem in Francis's mind. Bred a merchant's son, to carry on his father's business, he had had ambitions for renown in more distinguished fields. He had been deeply influenced by the chivalrous teaching of the romances, by the idealized knighthood of Roland and the paladins, the sentiment of chivalry which disguised the waning hold of feudal methods. Francis was drawn towards the old tradition, which the vigorous undertakings of his merchant kin were already superseding. That was his first conflict, and that perhaps which he had found on the way to Spoleto was disillusionment with knightly converse, turning out, as it did, to be little more than the grumblings of unpaid mercenaries and plans for increase of profit. And, disillusioned, he saw in his own dreams selfishness and snobbery: he had sometimes, he told Leo, turned away beggars asking alms for the love of God, when he would assuredly have listened to them had they asked in the name of a great count or baron.

Yet neither did he feel happy at the counting-table: the morality of the time was deeply suspicious of gain-getting. Society was thought of as in fixed ranks, and men did not pass from one to another. Serf, citizen, knight, so they were born, so they should remain, and their standard of life was fixed and known. This new trading for profit which enabled a Francis Bernardone to mix as an equal with nobles was a dubious innovation. The Church had always taught that pursuit of wealth was distraction of the spirit, now it was proving a menace also to the existing order. Trade, too, was the basis of town liberties, the source of Assisi's new-found independence; and the Church thought none the better of it for that: it was suspect and not altogether an easy matter of conscience. Francis knew the kind of criticisms his noble friends brought against it – harshness and avarice were the traits of his own father. The same problem that had worried Peter Waldo – the increase of wealth, with no increase in the evenness of its distribution, but rather new barriers built up to replace the old – worried Francis. He looked for Christian brotherhood in vain. His own riches, the luxury he had enjoyed and at times paraded, was a hindrance between him and his fellow-men, which he knew he must remove if he was to do them service.

It was at this time that he went on a pilgrimage to Rome, the classic remedy for spiritual unrest. There he would be free of all the difficult associations of Assisi, and might experiment in a new way of life. 'He desired,' Leo says, 'to be in a city as one unknown.' He came with the pilgrims to the shrine, and, when he saw how small were their offerings, he had one of his rare moments of impatience and flung all his purseful of money through the open grating with such a clatter of coin that all looked up in surprise at such liberality. Then, going outside, where the beggars waited on the steps, he persuaded one of them to lend him his rags, and the fastidious young merchant, famed for splendid dress, stood all day, clad in a filthy torn garment, begging among the beggars. He asked for alms in French, partly, perhaps, to disguise himself, partly because in his moments of excitement and enthusiasm he loved to speak it. It was the first 'doing violence to himself', which Celano, writing of him, sees as very needful in the making of a saint. He had begun to overcome disgust. It was no easy business for him; he had a nervous dread of all disfigurements. He used to dream that he had become hunchbacked and swollen, like beggars he knew in Assisi. *(Pl. II)*

One day, on his return from Rome, the great test came. Out riding, he met a leper, a common enough sight then: men hurried past, averting their eyes from the decaying hands and faces. Yet they were thought of as types of suffering humanity, men of sorrows . . . smitten of God. A writer contemporary with Francis, Cæsar of Heisterbach, has much to say of miracles attendant on charitable treatment of them, a service very pleasing to God; but the gorge rises even to read some of Cæsar's accounts of the disease's ravages – to look on it had always sickened Francis; he had always 'turned aside his face, stopping his nostrils with his hand' – the gesture of a man of more than common sensitiveness, capable of intense perception, capable now of a very purgatory in the training he had set himself. He dismounted, gave the leper alms and kissed his hand, receiving back the kiss of peace, defeating his own repugnance. From now on he visited regularly the little lazar house outside Assisi, and the lepers were to be a chief care of the brotherhood in its early days. Francis felt himself proved in the Lord's service. *(Pl. III)*

One day he went into the chapel of San Damiano to pray before the crucifix there. As he prayed and meditated on Christ's sufferings, and how little men were prepared to suffer for Him, it seemed to him that the painted figure spoke, giving a charge to him: 'My house is being destroyed; go therefore and repair it for Me.' Round him he saw the old chapel, dilapidated and crumbling, cared for by a poor priest only, with no money for oil for the lamps, far less for any work of restoration. And Francis, in his deep, simple devotion, first conceived of his work as the literal task of repairing the chapel. It was a natural thought for a man of his time. It is hard for us to realize how curiously direct were the unlettered men of the Middle Ages: reading little or not at all, they gave to action wide extensions of meaning, and they readily used it to express their longings. God was thought of very concretely; a feudal deity, whose land of Palestine must be restored to Him in no metaphorical sense. War against the infidel, the labour of a village hauling stones for an unnecessarily large cathedral, the abstinence of a monk cutting himself off from the world, the tangible bone of an apostle, to be seen and touched – these were things that men could understand; and we, to whom the written page means so much, will always misunderstand them if we forget it. For three years Francis devoted himself to the repair of churches, perceptible work on God's house, before he came to a wider realization of what its restoration might mean.

But first there was another renunciation to be made. Full of his new enthusiasm, Francis had left San Damiano, collected some cloth from the family store, and ridden over to Foligno to sell it; then, returning, he had presented the astonished priest with the money he had gained. Not unnaturally the good man was alarmed. He knew Francis and he knew his father, Peter. What would the latter think of this lavish alms? In the end he refused to accept it, and the bag of money was left unheeded on a window ledge of the little chapel. Peter had indeed been watching his son with growing uneasiness; now, the Foligno episode was too much for him. He sought for Francis to put an end to such follies, but the young man could not be found;

PLATE IV

ST FRANCIS BEATEN BY HIS FATHER

To St Francis, praying in the ruined church of S. Damiano, it seemed that the Christ on the crucifix spoke to him and bade him repair His house. Francis then taking some bales of cloth rode to Foligno, sold both the cloth and his horse, and, returning to Assisi, offered the money to the priest. But the priest, for fear of Francis's parents, refused the money, 'so the true despiser of monies cast the bag on the window sill, heeding it as little as dust.' His father, perhaps not surprisingly, was indignant at this transaction. 'And so, without any mercy, he shut him up for several days in a dark place, and, thinking to bend his spirit to his own will, urged him first by words and then by stripes and chains.' (Thomas of Celano *Legenda Prima*, CC.IV and V.)

he had hidden himself in a cave on the hillside, and here he remained for some time, and hither a friendly servant secretly brought out food to him from his father's house. Francis was as yet new to Christ's service, and he hesitated. Then one day he came out boldly, looking already unkempt as any hermit beggar, and went down to Assisi and his father's house. To Peter he was either a disobedient son or a lunatic: the cure for either was the same. Francis was put under lock and key, and his obduracy met by repeated floggings, till business took Peter at length from home. The lady Pica did not share her husband's views. She had always, it is said, even when Francis seemed most frivolous and irresponsible, replied to neighbours that 'by grace he should yet be the son of God'. Her influence had likely enough played a considerable part in her son's development. When her husband was gone she released him, and waited for the storm on Peter's return. *(Pl. IV)*

Francis now was prepared to resist. He had submitted to his father, and given him an opportunity to use all means of discipline and dissuasion with him, all with no result. There remained to stand his ground in open opposition. Peter, too, on his return, realized that blows and threats had failed, and he turned to a more sinister plan, citing Francis before the consuls of Assisi for having stolen money from him, a charge which with regard to the proceeds of Francis's sale at Foligno was true. The consuls summoned Francis, but were quite ready to shift their responsibility on Francis's plea that he was now 'a servant of God' and not within their jurisdiction – surprisingly ready, for Francis was still a layman and his clerkship lay only in his own sense of vocation and in the popular respect for any form of eccentric holiness. Bishop Guido, however, was not over-popular in the commune, and no doubt the civic authorities were pleased enough to transfer this family problem to him and to send Francis to the bishop's court. Guido had always in the past been kindly to him; he now bade him restore the money on his authority, for Francis had claimed that it had become the Church's property and that he could not give it back. Fortunately the bag of coins had lain undisturbed in the window-corner of San

Damiano, or else, more likely, had, on second thoughts, been put away safely by the priest. Then took place a moving scene, dear to later Italian painters. 'My lord,' said Francis to the bishop, 'I will gladly give back to him not only his money, but all my clothes which I have had of him.' So while the people wondered he went within the bishop's house, and returned naked and laid his clothes before his father. It was a formal act of renunciation of all his rights. 'Now,' said Francis, 'I shall say not my father Peter Bernardone, but only our Father which art in heaven.' The words are as if a legal formula, and were so meant. Some such act had probably been intended by Bernardone when he brought his son before the court; but there was a poignancy in Francis's naked body and in the characteristic simplicity of his literal-mindedness. The onlookers murmured as Bernardone picked up the clothes and went, and the bishop cast his cloak over Francis's naked shoulders. It was no pleasant scene: the rugged buildings of Assisi were very unlike the slender portico where Sassetta placed it when he painted it some hundred years later, and the sudden movement of conscience-stricken pity made by the father is also of the painter's imagining; there is no mention of it in the records; but already in Francis's actions there was a lyric fancy, which was to find true representation in the lines and gestures of the artists who painted his legend. They might romanticize the story, but the spirit was there at which they kindled.

CHAPTER THREE

THIS renunciation before the bishop was for Francis the decisive act committing him to his new life. Propertyless, without rank or station, he belonged now to no class; he had become a freeman of the brotherhood of all mankind. There remained, however, a sense of shame. In Assisi he was so well known; his old friends laughed at him; his father mocked or cursed him in the streets, and his prudent brother Angelo followed the paternal example. Francis as yet shunned such conspicuousness. He sought the woods and hillsides. For a time he served as a scullion in a neighbouring monastery, which gave him little kindness, not knowing whom it was entertaining unawares; then he moved on to Gubbio, where he had a friend whom he could trust and talk with, and he, always friendly and sympathetic, must have needed such talk more than any alms; then back to San Damiano, and the task which still called him of church building.

For some three years, or the best part of them, Francis worked at this labour, going up to Assisi to beg for stones, or oil for the lamps once a chapel was restored. It was only a few years since the men of Assisi had built their city walls – work in which Francis must have shared. That they had shown such civic eagerness, while allowing their chapels to decay, was easily seen as a reproach; and many of them were soon ready to turn to and help him. Francis sang while he worked – his odd mixture of praise to God and the latest French *jongleur* song. Already many felt his persuasiveness; and it was well, too, for Assisi to have a local holy man. Soon some were boasting of him; and San Damiano, the larger church of San Pietro, the little chapel of Sta Maria della Porziuncola – all were repaired, and perhaps others too, for there seems to have been a whole school of buildings grown up round Francis's efforts. He meanwhile continued the conquest of himself. Living at San Damiano, he saw how the old priest grew to care more and more for him, and how he would prepare special dishes for him that he knew he liked. This was no true poverty, and Francis determined to live on what he could obtain in alms. The first day that he brought himself to beg in Assisi, and then sat down in a corner to feed on a mess of fragments at which his stomach turned, was a new step forward. Another time, begging for oil, he saw lamps burning, well supplied, and went towards them. But it was a feast of his old friends – such a one as he had often presided over – and he hesitated, perhaps to spare their embarrassment as much as his own – not, however, for long; entering, he owned to the cowardice that had momentarily stayed him from God's work. And all the time he continued visiting the lepers.

It was when worshipping in the little chapel of the Porziuncola, in the early spring of 1209, that Francis came to a new conclusion as to the work to which he was called. The Gospel for the day was from the tenth chapter of St Matthew: 'And as ye go, preach, saying, The kingdom of heaven is at hand. . . . Provide neither gold, nor silver, nor brass in your purses, nor scrip for your journey, neither two coats, neither shoes, nor yet staves: for the workman is worthy of his meat. . . . And when ye come into an house, salute it. And if the house be worthy, let your peace come upon it.' Francis had received some education from the priests of San Giorgio, one of the churches in Assisi. He could write, probably better in his counting-house days than when he wrote, somewhat awkwardly, the letter to Leo which survives. He knew some Latin, and could read the Bible; but there his education ended. He could be thought of as 'unlettered', one who had some little skill for ordinary affairs, but had followed no course of studies. He had wondered once, Leo tells us, whether he should study and become learned; but, thinking it over, he felt called to a direct way of imitation rather than any reasoning about God's will. When he read the Gospels, he used often to open them at random, and there read, seeking guidance, not having that close familiarity which easily finds a particular text. The passages read in the offices of the Church were those best known to him. As he listened now to the words from St Matthew, he saw in them a new relevance to the problems he was pondering upon. In his last Testament, looking back at this moment of illumination, he wrote: 'No one showed me what I should do, but the Most High Himself revealed to me that I should live according to the rule of the Gospel.' Going to the priest, he talked with him about the passage read, testing his own understanding of it and finding in it an answer to his desires.

From now on he discarded his sandals and walked barefoot, without staff or wallet, having only one tunic girded with a piece of rope. The Franciscan dress was in being, and the Franciscan way of life entered upon. 'The Lord give you peace' was his greeting, the familiar one of the itinerant hermit, and from that he would enlarge on the contrariness of division, very simply with no eloquence, but there was something in his words and the way he said them, and the life he led, that pierced, as Leo puts it, 'into the marrow of the heart.' It was with this beginning of preaching that others came to join Francis.

First of all Bernard of Quintavalle and Peter Catani. Bernard was a well-to-do Assisian, whose house, close to the cathedral square, is still pointed out today; he had sometimes lodged Francis there, and had long discussions with him. One night he told him that he had resolved to distribute his goods to the poor and join him in his life of poverty. Peter Catani, a doctor of law who had studied at Bologna, had also made some such approach to Francis. Next day the three of them went to the church of St Nicholas. The book of the Gospels lay on the altar: first they prayed, and then Francis opened it, searching for the passages on which his assurance rested.

He came on the words of Matthew: 'If thou wouldst be perfect, go and sell all thou hast, and give to the poor'; then those of Luke: 'Take nothing for your journey'; then, again in Matthew: 'Then Jesus said unto His disciples, If any man will come after Me, let him deny himself, and take up his cross, and follow Me.' 'My brothers,' Francis said to them, 'this is our Life and Rule, and that of all who shall wish to join our company. Go, therefore, and fulfil that ye have heard.' Bernard and Peter went and distributed their goods in the market-place, and came, clad only in peasants' tunics such as Francis wore, to live with him under shelters of branches in the woods round the Porziuncola.

These were men of substance and learning, seeking, like Francis, a new freedom of life through great renunciation. The next disciple was very different, and a man who in his difference was to have great influence on the Order. Giles was a peasant, simple, unlettered, but shrewd-witted and ready-tongued, and pensive with the intuition of a

PLATE V

ST FRANCIS AND RUFINO PREACHING NAKED IN ASSISI

St Francis ordered Brother Rufino to go and preach in Assisi, but Rufino begged to be excused. Then St Francis, because he had been unwilling to obey, ordered him to go and preach in Assisi, 'stripped and wearing nothing but your under garment'. But when Rufino departed, St Francis repented of his harshness, hurried after him and, stripping himself also, joined him in preaching, speaking of the nakedness and humiliation of the Passion of our Lord.' In the story as the 'Fioretti' tells it, they were stripped to their undergarments; but to Arthur Boyd the theme of nakedness is more stressed and complete, and Brother Rufino instead of mounting the pulpit steps cowers unhappily, while Francis, unashamed, is transfigured in ecstacy. (Fioretti C.29)

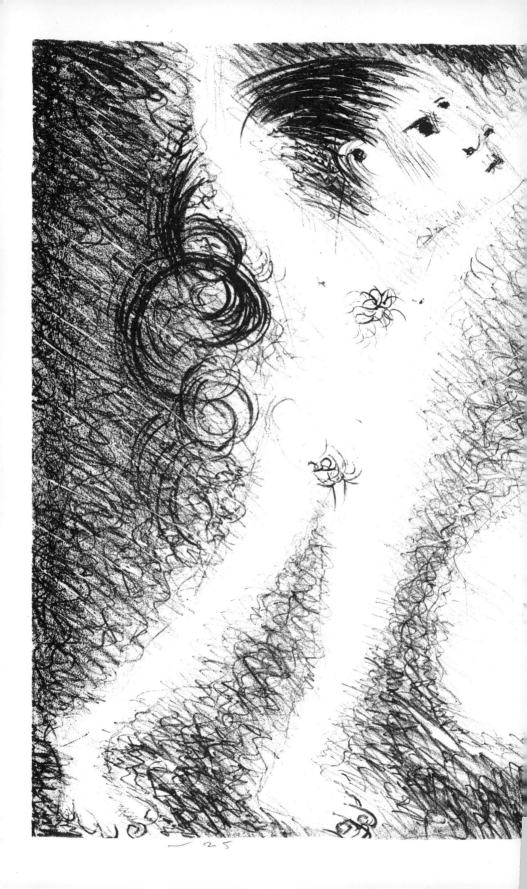

country-dweller who feels God through nature: he was to become, with Francis's aid, 'a master in the science of the soul'. He came through the woods one day, and knelt by Francis, saying, 'Brother, I would be with you.' And Francis saw in him a kindred spirit, and, taking him back to Bernard, said, 'The Lord has sent us a good brother.'

It was with these three companions that the missionary journeys began: Bernard and Peter one way, Francis and Giles another into the Mark of Ancona, Francis singing as ever his French songs and already saying how 'Our Religion (a religion being the term for an order) is a net which holds the great fish, but lets go the little' – meaning that only the great-hearted would remain in it. Francis does not as yet seem to have preached in any formal sense: he had of course no licence to sermonize, but as they came to villages his greeting of 'peace' would ring out, and he talked with all who would pause by the road or in the market, exhorting them to love and fear God and do penance for their sins. Leo, however, tells us that the way of penitence was unknown, and many thought Giles and Francis either drunk or mad, 'for their way of life seemed too hard to be borne.'

They returned, therefore, unreinforced; but, back at the Porziun-cola, others from Assisi joined them: Sylvester; Morico, a brother of the Crucigieri, an order that tended lepers; John of Campello, who in the end fell into exaggerations of piety; Philip, an able speaker; and the fame of their doings must have been spread by the missions, for from Rieti came one Angelo Tancredi, a man of knightly birth, whose coming was particularly welcome to Francis for Angelo was 'adorned with all courtesy', and he seemed to be a fulfilment of Francis's youthful ideals.

The growing community aroused interest and admiration, but also criticism. It began early: when Bernard and Peter divided their goods in the Piazza San Giorgio, a priest – Sylvester – had protested, saying that they had all freely, on the grounds of his poverty, contributed stones for Francis's rebuilding, and here he was giving away riches; it was only right that he should first pay them; at which Francis took two handfuls of money from Bernard and gave them to the priest, saying, 'Have you now your payment in full?' It was this same Sylvester who soon after joined the Order, for the words and glance of Francis had searched his heart, and he knew that his protest came from greed rather than zeal for justice. But there were others to bring forward similar arguments; when the brothers came up the hill to beg in Assisi, they were not always welcome. They had given up their own goods, they were told, to devour those of other men. Bishop Guido felt called upon to intervene, and expressed his doubts to Francis that this absolute poverty was too hard a rule and should be mitigated. To whom Francis replied, in words of great importance for his whole outlook: 'My lord, if we should have possessions, we should need arms to protect ourselves. For thence arise plaints and lawsuits, and for this cause the love of God and of our neighbour is commonly hindered in many ways, and so we do not wish to possess any temporal goods in the world.'

Poverty is the great vehicle of Francis's teaching, and, in his early days, its main content, hard but necessary for us to understand. In the forefront is the apostolic command to 'take nothing' with them. 'I must live,' said Francis, 'according to the rule of the Gospels.' And by that rule he meant exact adherence to Christ's instructions and the pattern of Christ's own life. That Jesus held any rigorist view of poverty such as that of Francis is not explicit anywhere in His teaching, and when the papacy, a hundred years later, condemned the Franciscan doctrine its exegesis was the sounder. Francis accepted a traditional view, in no way based on study or essays in interpretation, but it agreed entirely with these direct commands, which seemed to be the centre of the Gospel teach-ing: 'Sell all thou hast. . . . leave father and mother and wife and child . . . give thy cloak also.' Such a life had been led by Christ and the Apostles, and only those leading some such life could hope to evangelize, to draw men once more to God, in this age where 'the way of penitence' was utterly unknown. To the young merchant of Assisi, half ashamed of the traders' victory over the old nobility, puzzled by the new luxuries of life in which only the few shared, pursuit of wealth was the great enemy. Francis perceived how this new power, which some shrewd deal brought to a merchant, separated him only the more from the worker whose labour he required. The old days of a self-sufficing economy, when a locality toiled for its own upkeep and all barter was in kind, were simpler, friendlier times than now when men traded at a distance with unknown clients, and hard metal was all that passed between them – metal that no friar must ever touch, which was 'of less account than dung'. Once when a coin was given them and a brother, with no ill intention, took it up, Francis bade him take the coin in his mouth and place it in excrement by the wayside. For it was through the increasing circulation of such coins that came the new systems against which Francis sought a Christian protest of voluntary renouncement.

Very shortly after Francis's death, a small pamphlet was written – the *Sacrum Commercium* or *Holy Converse* – in praise of poverty, and to confirm the brethren in the pursuit of it, for it is 'the foundation and guardian of every virtue and the most excellent and readiest way of coming into God's presence'. These pages hold much of the Franciscan secret; the joy that is so lively throughout them comes from the true carelessness of those for whom the world holds no hostages. The poor are indeed blessed in spirit and are not anxious. No one has ever equalled Francis as an example of happiness: the Provençal songs went on praising God in light-heartedness, through hunger and cold and all men mean by misery, through aching bodily pain and harder disappointment of mind. While he lay ill and near dying, he could write his great outburst of joy, the Canticle of the Sun, praising all nature for its bounty. He who had no ties was bound to the whole world, and his abject state seemed to him, as indeed it was, the highest romance, the service of his Lady Poverty, among whose knights alone true courtesy, his favourite word, was found. There is the white heat of poetry in Francis's words and gestures which dazzles sometimes, and lifts us to a feeling of holiness sooner than we deserve it, for most of us stand condemned by his enthusiasm. In the *Sacrum*

Commercium there is a chapter of how Avarice called herself Pru-
dence, saying: 'Why stand ye here all the day idle, taking no thought
for the morrow? What hinders you from having the necessities of
life, if you abstain from superfluities? For if all things needful were
at hand, you would then have peace and quiet to work out your
own and other men's salvation. Would it not be acceptable to
God if you had wherewith to give to the poor? By refusing the good
things offered, you defraud the givers of their reward. Sin does not
lie in things, it is in the mind ... to the good all things are good.'

These, or some of them, were serious arguments, and there are
others, or other wording of them, which could be used today. It is
time to examine them more closely, leaving the bewildering glory
of Francis's magnetism. First of all, Francis had no intention that
his followers should stand idle: 'The brethren who know how to
work' – so runs the Rule – 'shall work and exercise that craft which
they know, if it be not against their soul's salvation, and they can
exercise it honestly. For the Prophet says, "Because that thou shalt
eat the labours of thy hands, blessed art thou and it shall be well with
thee"; and the Apostle says, "He who will not work neither let him
eat ..." and for their labours they may receive whatever is needful,
except money. And should it be necessary (i.e. should they not
obtain what is needful) they shall ask alms like other brothers.' And
again in his final Testament: 'I worked with my hands, and so I
desire to work, and I firmly desire that all the other brethren work in
some honest employment. Let those who know not, learn how to
work, not through desire to receive the price of their labour, but for
example's sake and to repel idleness. And when the price of our
labour is not given us, let us have recourse to the table of the Lord,
begging alms from door to door.' There is here an apostolic echo,
some memory of Paul the tent-maker, but there seems to be also
some confusion of thought. When Francis recalls how he worked
with his hands, he must have been thinking of the repairing of
the churches: that was done in the conviction that it was God's
work, and that the labourer 'was worthy of his meat'; a man so
working, whether it is building of stones or the seeking of souls on a

missionary journey, may rightly take the support given him – that must be the belief of all feeling themselves called to an urgent mission. But this is a different justification than work for work's sake, to repel idleness; that comes from the discipline of the Benedictine monastic rule. Consistency of thought, however, never interested Francis; idleness he knew was dangerous; to live on alms had its dangers also: if the brothers could exchange their work for sus⁄ tenance, well and good, it was honest employment and a service to the community; but there were demands on them for a greater service which would have no market value, which could not be postponed to any material needs, for which they must eat at the table of the Lord. His Religion, his Order, was not to Francis an economic system. He never considered what would happen if the whole world became Franciscan, nor ever imagined that it would, and he planned for no earthly millennium complete in itself. He had no schemes of communal production; he sought only to guard against new temptations by voluntary redistribution: to him brotherly love meant tireless discontent while any man remained poorer than he was. 'Always,' he said, 'I have taken less than I needed lest I should defraud other poor men of their share'; and at the same time he would teach the sufficiency of God and the joy of the way of penitence – 'Great shame it is to me when I find anyone poorer than I am, since I have chosen poverty for my Lady.' And in this profession of poverty the thought might sometimes lack consis⁄ tency, but no compromise was to be tolerated. They were acting a parable as monasticism acted a parable, and as the crusades, in their ideal aspect, were a parable also: here was the way of life shown out as men without books could understand it, a greater mystery play. But the players must be action⁄perfect, and Francis above all must be their prompter. There can be little question that calmly and quite consciously he shortened his life by refusing all alleviations which his ill health required, lest it should lead to some departure from his perfect concept of the Order. Once when, in winter, at Rieti they lined his tunic with some patches against the cold, he tore them off again, saying, 'Though it be needful for my body to have a lined

tunic, yet must I consider other brethren to whom the same is
needful, and who perhaps cannot have it. . . . I must bear the want
that they bear, that seeing this in me, they may suffer more patiently.'
Later, in his time of illness, when a brother again secretly sewed a
small foxskin on the inside of his tunic, Francis unwillingly wore it
for a time, but only on condition that some of the skin was sewn
outside also, so that all might see it was there. In great things and in
little he was constant: refusing to spare himself, dreading any
pretence, or suddenly, with humorous ingenuity, asking the cooking
brother if it were not taking thought for the morrow, when he
soaked the dry beans overnight. But to his followers Francis counselled moderation: 'Let each consider his own nature; because
one needs less sustenance than another, let not the brother who needs
more be held to imitation of him who needs less, but let him consider his own nature and give it that nourishment which it requires
that it may serve the spirit. For we must abstain from too great
abstinence as from too great superfluity.' When a brother fainted
from fasting, Francis came and ate with him, and made the others
do likewise, lest he should feel shame at having to eat alone: and
when another brother was ill, Francis took him down to a vineyard
and they ate grapes together. 'Brother body' should not be over-
wearied, but should not be allowed to become slothful – 'the goad is
for the sluggish ass'. Such was his theory of asceticism. If Francis
himself died worn out at the age of forty-four, many of his companions long survived him and were old men when they died.

In Assisi there might be criticism, but the band at the Porziuncola
did not decrease in numbers. In spring of 1210 there were eleven
disciples with Francis (unless the number has been made to fit
a sacred parallel); and as men questioned their aims, and he himself
would always accept question in all humility, he determined to seek
the advice of a greater authority than the Bishop of Assisi, and to subject his schemes to Rome.

CHAPTER FOUR

INNOCENT III, the ablest politician of his time, was in the summer of 1210 in the full course of his activities, immersed in problems and diplomacies of which Francis could have no conception. There is a tradition that 'the poor penitents of Assisi' succeeded, by persuasion or chance, in being admitted to the papal presence, but, unsponsored and unexplained, were hastily dismissed as a meaning-less interruption. Not that Innocent was without sympathy for simple piety or unaware of what forms such piety was taking: with his rare combination of administrative and pastoral gifts, he saw the issues of his day in terms both of ecclesiastical expediency and personal salvation. He had already given a rule to the Humiliati of Milan, emphasizing the monastic ideal, but leaving them their mixed community, even their preaching, for, he told them, 'the Spirit ought not to be quenched'. Since then, it is true, events in Languedoc had reached a crisis. Innocent was now stamping out heresy by war, and had had to abandon earlier schemes of conversion through the peaceful mission of Dominic Guzman. He might be expected to be harsher now with popular, undisciplined religious movements; and the policy of the curia was to encourage existing orders rather than to sanction new, which, insufficiently supervised, easily fell into faulty beliefs. Poverty could be practised in some Carthusian or Cistercian foundation, where there were adequate safeguards against its more dangerous implications. Yet Innocent knew that this craving for apostolic imitation contained a necessary stimulus for Christendom. Francis stood for much that the Pope desired. Later he was to say that he had dreamed how a little man such as Francis supported the falling Lateran. He could hardly be expected to devote time and care to examining all stray enthusiasts, but he was capable, proud nobleman of the Campagna that he was, of understanding Francis's aims.

Fortunately for the Assisians, their bishop happened to be in Rome at the time. Through his good agency they gained the interest of the Cardinal of Sta Sabina, who of all the college was best known for piety and virtuous life. The personality of Francis at once impressed him, but the vague collection of texts, the few rules about work, and going unprovided through the world, which was all the Rule Francis had drawn up, hardly suggested an efficient and reliable

PLATE VI

ST FRANCIS MAKES BROTHER MASSEO TURN ROUND AND ROUND

The 'Fioretti' tells how St Francis and Brother Masseo came to a place where three roads met and Masseo asked by which road they should go. 'St Francis replied "By that which God wills". "And how," said Brother Masseo, "can we know the will of God." St Francis replied: "By the sign that I shall shew you; when I command you by the merit of holy obedience that at this cross road, on the spot where your feet are placed, you spin yourself round and round, as children do, and do not stop from turning yourself till I tell you to".' Masseo turned himself till he was giddy and fell down, but even then St Francis said nothing, so he rose and continued till St Francis stopped him. He was then facing the road to Siena and that was the road they took. (Fioretti C.10)

15— 25

group of men. Francis found himself faced with disappointments and delays, in which it seemed that the whole scheme might founder, and in which all his perseverance was required. He was called before Innocent, and spoke to him with all the picturesque vigour of his beloved romances: the story of a fair woman in the desert, poor but lovely, who bore sons to a great king, and when they were grown sent them to his court. 'Be not ashamed, my sons, for that you are poor, for you are sons of a great king,' and the king, recognizing them, said: 'My sons and heirs you are; fear not. If strangers are fed at my table, by a greater right must I nourish these for whom all my possessions are lawfully kept.' This was the parable Francis told to Innocent. 'I am that poor woman, Holy Father, who sends my sons to court.' It was as the teller of legends, the man who so gaily spoke of God, that Francis won Innocent.

But the Pope was won only to a guarded approval. It is difficult to be certain what was the exact Rule which he authorized, for in its primitive form it has not come down, and we know it only from the 'First Rule' drawn up in 1221, which was the Rule of 1210 with additions made in the intervening years. It seems clear, however, that Innocent made certain stipulations: the brothers might go out proclaiming God's peace and calling to repentance, but it was no general licence to preach and expound doctrine, and before they were accounted of the Order all must promise obedience to Francis, as Francis promised it to him. Finally the brothers were given the narrow tonsure – not the full tonsure of the monk, but that which marked men in minor orders, and it was probably at this time that Francis himself was ordained deacon. In this successful obtaining of papal assent, the Cardinal of Sta Sabina had counted for much. 'Let us beware,' he said, in consistory, 'lest we offend against the Gospel of Christ.'

The journey home was to provide a curious commentary on the fears and enthusiasms of the Roman discussions. North of Rome the road lies through barren hill country, where a traveller might go long without meeting anyone or coming to a house. The brothers had made no sufficient preparation for the journey, and night

overtook them in a deserted spot, faint for lack of food, nor next day
was there much hope of finding any; then, when some were sinking
with exhaustion, a traveller came, and gave them bread in alms, and
wondering who he was and trusting more than ever in God's grace,
they came on to Orte. Here, tired out, they halted some days, in an
old Etruscan tomb above the town, some of the brothers going
down each day to beg in Orte itself. It was a lonely and forsaken
spot, and at it there took place a debate of a most momentous nature
for the future of the Order. Constant advice at Rome had been that
they should attach themselves to an existing order; the orthodox
cœnobitic life, groups of hermits living in poverty together, had been
stressed, and the value of the contemplative life expounded to them,
finding in them very ready listeners. St Francis was endowed with
great powers of prayer: it was his constant activity, and his deep
concentration on it was one of the clearest memories of him. He
talked often about prayer to his followers, in particular warning
them against ostentation in it: he himself, if others were by, hid his
head in his cloak and kept still so that his praying passed unnoticed;
or he rose very quietly and prayed in the night, though were he alone
he would pray with groans and sighs, beating his breast. He was,
too, very regular in the saying of the Canonical Hours, always,
however ill he was, reciting them kneeling or standing, and always
with complete devotion of mind. Once, when he was praying, his
eyes fell on a pot he had been making, for he had some skill in that,
and his thoughts flew back to some problem in connection with it;
but when he had finished praying, he threw it on to the fire, saying,
'Let us be ashamed of trivial fancies when we are speaking to the
great King.' For such prayers the hermit's life offered unique
opportunity, and Francis often yearned for it. In the woods on
Mount Subasio, there were some rock caves by a stream, and here,
at the Carceri, as it was called, the brothers were to have a constant
and beloved retreat. Many of them – Sylvester, Rufino, Giles in his
later years – lived mainly as hermits, and were known for rare gifts of
mystical experience. It was a very grave discussion, then, in the cave
at Orte, when they wondered 'whether they ought to live among

men or betake them to solitary places'. There seemed no selfishness in such withdrawal, for prayer to Francis could not have seemed a self-regarding act: rather in refusing it, in staying in the world rather than separating themselves from it, as the monkish tradition taught, there was a gesture of humility. They were simple folk who must gain souls for God by the imitation of His actions, by the acting of His words, rather than by the ardours of His undistracted contemplation. Much of Francis's originality lies in his teaching about the training needful for prayer, of perseverance when the 'grace of devotion' came not, and of the greatness of the effort required. 'Since no one,' said Giles, his pupil, 'can enter upon the contemplative life unless he hath first been faithfully and devoutly practised in the active, it behoveth that the active be pursued with toil and all solicitude'; and this same Giles once said that if he had achieved anything in prayer, it was because he was a great robust fellow, and able to endure prolonged and heavy labour. Leaving Orte, lest by longer stay they might seem to lay claim to ownership of the cave, they came by Spoleto, with its memories of the expedition to war, back to Assisi.

Returned, Francis devoted himself with new energy to preaching; despite the limitation to a call to penitence, he was now 'a true preacher, confirmed by apostolic authority'. We have various accounts of his discourses from those who heard him; he was essentially an impromptu speaker; when he prepared his speech carefully, he often forgot it, and found the effort to remember hindered him; it was the manner that counted more than the matter. He preached 'in homely and unlearned language ... he would hint in a few words at what was unspeakable, and, mingling ardent gestures and movements with his words, trans- ported his hearers wholly to heavenly things.' Once, when he preached before Honorius III, carried away by what he was saying, he moved his feet as though dancing, to the alarm of Cardinal Ugolino, who feared his simplicity might be despised; he lacked presence; austerities had left their mark on him; soon his eyes were to be dimmed and bloodshot, but the voice was clear and

musical, and in his expression there was conviction of joy and peace
beyond gainsaying. This smiling prophet, singing and dancing
God's praises, was irresistibly infectious in his gaiety of soul. A
learned listener once said of him: 'I never remember what words he
uses, and if I do they do not seem to me to be the same.' 'He was a
man,' says Celano, 'most eloquent, of cheerful countenance.' Now,
back from Rome, he was frequently invited to preach in San Rufino,
the Cathedral of Assisi. We have no record of his actual teaching,
but undoubtedly it was a call to peace, and again and again the
warning not to place their trust in temporal riches. A picture, which
he draws in one of his surviving letters, is that of the rich man's
deathbed, where the dying man assigns all his goods to his family,
so that he cannot obey the command of the Church to make resti-
tution for his frauds and deceptions: it is a curious parable, a *genre*
piece, with accurate knowledge of legal details, and with the horror
rather in the grumblings of his kin than in the devil who takes
away his soul, a grim death rather than a lurid one. The disgust at
sin is stronger than the fear of hell fire; and, above all, there is
Francis's particular hatred of legalism. Law is for him always the
necessary evil, the compromise with an unchristian world; and
when, in his own Order, such laws and compromise were to be
demanded, it was bitter indeed for him.

With the policies of the commune Francis does not seem to have
mixed himself. The treaty of five years earlier with Perugia had
been ineffective, and the background of skirmishes and castle-
burning continued; but in 1210, when a new papal-imperial war
was brooding over Umbria, Assisi seems finally to have readmitted
its exiles, and a new pact was signed, by which the citizens pledged
themselves to prevent divisions in the city and that neither
party, 'the greater' nor 'the lesser', should make separate terms with
pope or king or other city; once more, with the return of further
rebel nobles, there are long details of feudal dues and services, and
questions of franchises, not altogether to the loss of the nobles.
'Majores' and 'Minores': the terms are common ones in Italy of the
early thirteenth century. At a later date they would describe the

wealthy capitalist merchant and the poor wage labourer, protected
by no guild, or, at the best, by a feeble one; but in Assisi in 1210 the
Majores are still the feudal class, with whom the rising merchants
eagerly associate themselves. The Minores are the lesser trading folk
who have been less skilful in their enterprises, who still make for
small markets and have missed the wider ventures of foreign trade;
below them are the real 'little men,' the toilers, but they have no
voice in treaty making. 'Brothers Minor,' Francis began, at this
time, to call his Order, but with no reference to civic politics. The
pact as a measure of peace must have pleased him, but there is no
evidence that his preaching disposed them to it. His 'Minores'
were to be lesser than the least; his teaching was of individual
penitence rather than reforms and treaties: he was not afraid to go,
even, and preach in hated Perugia – Perugia of his imprisonment –
where in the great square the knights rode up and down on their
chargers and he could hardly make his voice heard above the din.
'Ye ought to be kinder to your neighbours, and more thankful to
God,' he told them.

PLATE VII

ST FRANCIS HOLDING ST CLARE'S HAIR

'*And so going forth, leaving the house, the city and her kindred, she went eagerly to S. Maria di Porziuncula, where the brothers, keeping vigil in the church, welcomed the holy maid by torchlight. And laying aside all worldly vanity of Babylon, she gave there forthwith a bill of divorcement from the world, and leaving the tresses of her shorn hair in the hands of the friars completely abandoned all adornment.' (Legenda S. Clarae C.IV)*

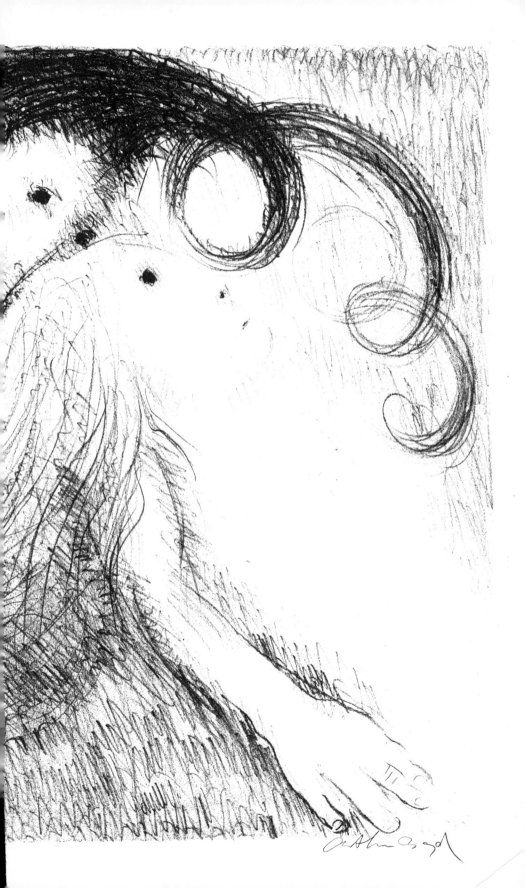

CHAPTER FIVE

THE little group of twelve had at first on their return gone to Rivo Torto, by the leper settlement of Sta Maria Maddalena; here, in a ruined cowshed, they found a resting-place, and Francis chalked out on the wooden walls a space for each brother, so that, though cramped for space, they should all come in and dwell together, not some lie without, hoping the others should have greater comfort. Then one day a neighbouring peasant, the owner of the tumbledown shelter, boorishly drove his ass into it while the brothers were at prayer, with some loud remarks to his beast about the comfortable dwelling he'd find there. It was discourtesy, of all things abhorrent to Francis; and we get in Leo's story of it one of those rare flashes of anger. As the man talked to his ass, so that the brothers should hear him, Francis rose to his feet: 'I know, brethren, that God has not called us to provide stabling for an ass, nor meeting-places for men, but that we should always preach unto men the way of salvation, giving salutary counsels, and in especial that we ought to devote ourselves unto prayer and thanksgiving.' So they left Rivo Torto; and Francis, thinking of his care for churches – and still he went round working in them, sweeping them out, and carving wood for their decoration, and when he became frailer he was to make the wafers for consecration – sought a chapel where they might meet and pray; and the Abbot of Monte Subasio offered him the little chapel of the Porziuncola, St Mary of the Little Portion – offered it him not as a gift, for Francis would have no proprietary right, and for their use of it every year they sent a basket of fish to the monastery. Round it, they built shelters of boughs built against the tree trunks, for it was still woodland then in the valley below Assisi.

It is the idyllic time of the Order's history. Numbers were growing, and already the great names in Franciscan history were gathered round their founder, but not yet were the numbers a problem. St Francis, wandering in Umbria, drew men to him, but as yet the ends of the world were not come upon Assisi. There was still room for them in the woodland, even when none had gone out with the message. Brother Giles was the most energetic of the missionaries. He went to Compostella with Bernard of Quintavalle, and there were few of the Italian shrines that he did not visit – Rome, Bari, Monte Gargano – always working his way, helping the harvesters, making baskets of rushes, selling fresh water in an east-coast port, burying the dead. Even when he stayed with a cardinal in Rome he would go down and work in the kitchen in return for a loaf of bread; and all the time he had shrewd comments and advice on everything, and already men were treasuring 'the golden sayings of brother Giles'; and it was Giles who first of the friars crossed the sea and came to Jerusalem. And now Francis had with him the three companions who were in later days to set down their memories of him – Leo, Rufino, and Angelo: Leo, whom Francis called 'Pecorello di Dio', the little sheep of God, who was to be the saint's secretary and afterwards to write of his teaching; Rufino, the Assisian noble, retiring and halting in speech, who preferred the quiet of the lonely Carceri to missionary journeys, whom once Francis ordered by holy obedience to preach in Assisi, and, when he expostulated, bade him leave his tunic, and go in his breeches only to the church and so preach half naked; but, when Rufino went Francis repented of his severity and, throwing off his tunic, followed to the church, where to a gaping crowd Rufino, the former noble-man, naked to the waist, was stammering out the Franciscan message. Francis, naked like him, came beside him and poured out such a heartfelt praise of poverty that all wept who heard him *(Pl. V)*;

Leo meanwhile had followed with the two discarded tunics, so that they could depart clothed once more: Rufino was one to whom much of the Franciscan life was very difficult. Angelo it was who had been a knight in the world; and now Francis had another special joy. A *jongleur* came to join him, a maker of songs, known as 'The King of Verses,' crowned as such by the young Frederick in Palermo, and Francis called him Brother Pacifico. Brother Masseo, the handsome, was the best preacher, the man of common sense, whom Francis loved to have with him, and mocked a little, bidding him turn round and round till he told him to stop and then follow the road before him, when Masseo would rather have discussed the virtues of the different routes; the *Fioretti* has a further tale of how once when Francis and Masseo were talking of poverty, the fervour of the saint raised Masseo into the air and cast him a spear's length from him. Juniper, the simpleton, most literal of all the brothers, was always in some misunderstanding, always cheerful and generous, who sat on a seesaw outside Rome playing with the children till his pious admirers tired of waiting for him – the most Franciscan of them all in his selfless humility, whom Clare loved in particular and called 'the plaything of God'. *(Pl. VI)*

And Clare herself. It was in the Holy Week of 1212 that this daughter of a noble Assisian house, a girl of some eighteen years, came down to the Porziuncola, where Francis cut off her long hair in sign of admission to his Order, and then took her to the neigh- bouring monastery of San Paolo. For both of them it was a step of great daring: he, on his side, had no authority to admit women, nor to administer vows to them – it might well bring against the brothers all the indignation of Assisi, for Clare's family had much influence; she, on her side, had to face the wrathful remonstrance of her kin, knowing that Francis had no refuge to give her. *(Pl. VII)*

In the chronicles, this story of Clare and Francis, and later his friendship with the Roman lady, Jacopa of Settesoli, are guardedly handled. The monkish tradition regarded women as a source of temptation, and Celano and Bonaventura both hasten over these episodes in Francis's life, not, be it well understood, that they them⁄

selves suspected them, but for fear lest they should give scandal to the general public. Celano writes of 'that honeyed poison, familiarity with women, which leads even holy men astray', and almost apologizes for Francis, introducing a story of how he once said that there were only two women whom he knew by sight (for Celano can hardly overlook Clare and Jacopa entirely), and that while talking to women he never looked at them, but kept his eyes bent down, and other words to this effect. In such sayings Celano is voicing the ideals of his time; he cannot, in fact, refrain from bursting into praise of Francis's wisdom, forgetting the usual objectivity of his narrative. 'Well said, father,' he exclaims, 'for the sight of them makes no one holy. Well said, I repeat, for they bring no light, but much loss, were it but loss of time, hindering those who

PLATE VIII

ST FRANCIS AND THE HARLOT

When St Francis was travelling in the lands of the Sultan he came to an inn, where a woman tempted him to sin. 'Then St Francis said "If you wish that I consent, I wish that you also consent to me." She said "I accept what you say. Let us go then and prepare a bed." St Francis said "Come with me, and I will show you the fairest bed." And he led her to a great fire which there was in that house. And in fervour of spirit he undressed himself and lay down naked as in a bed on that red hot hearth. And calling to her he said "Undress yourself and make haste to enjoy this splendid bed, flowering and wonderful, for here you must be, if you would obey me." But the fire injured St Francis not at all and he joyfully lay glowing upon the hearth as upon flowers and that woman seeing such wonders and amazed not only was turned from the filth of her sins but also from the darkness of unbelief to the Lord Jesus Christ.' (Actus Beatus Francisci et Sociorum Ejus, C.XXVII)

15—25

would be bent on the arduous journey, and would look upon the Countenance that is full of all grace.' Such sayings are part of the strange story of chastity, with its heights and depths. In popular moralizing of Francis's day, when the Church demanded but did not always obtain celibacy from its clergy, women were the chief danger to the soul. Here and there some of the new sects, such as the Humil-iati claimed a freer ideal of comradeship; and here, as at so many points, early Franciscanism has common ground with them. For of the standpoint that Celano attributes to him there is no trace in Francis's own pronouncements: women, he laid down later, were not to be admitted to the Porziuncola; but he was thinking then of friars tending on themselves, of service rather than pleasure, and he never thought to let this ruling hinder Jacopa's last visit to him. 'He specially loved,' Leo says, 'the fairness and cleanness of decency, and wished the friars to have modest eyes; teaching them that when they looked on a woman they looked on the spouse of Christ.' A legend, again in the *Fioretti,* tells how he converted a prostitute by bidding her lie beside him on the hot stones of the hearth before a blazing fire, where he remained unharmed, while any other would have been scorched and burned. This is a far other matter, whether coming down to us through fact or fable, than the timid purity which fears the wiles of the Devil. Francis assuredly was not unaware of the dangers that beset a celibate order; love of women and family life were part of the sacrifice in his perfect poverty; but already many were coming to him who could not leave all worldly ties, who sought to follow his precepts while living and loving and possessing in the more normal way of the world. And amongst these followers were many women, of whom Francis, with his almost feminine sensitiveness, had a keen understanding; who, in return, often seemed best able to understand him: without Clare and Jacopa the Franciscan story would have been very different, and we should have known it far less fully. *(Pl. VIII)*

Clare's father was one Favarone, who with his elder brother Monaldo had been amongst the rebel nobles who sided with Perugia: their fief of Monte Aldone lay between the warring cities, exposed to all the plots and schemes of the time. Clare, with other girls of her own age and standing, seems to have spent an émigré childhood living in Perugia; and it was only after the half-peace of 1205 that she was brought back to Assisi, not to a feudal castle, but to one of the new houses within the city walls, on the cathedral square, and described as 'the finest in the city'. She lived among the stress of decline and change, and these feudal ladies, who had seen their castles pulled down and known exile, found consolation and some stability in pious practices. Clare's mother, Ortolana, was much given to pilgrimages, and had been to Jerusalem, and her friends were like-minded: their words or their daughters' memories of them are preserved for us in the process for the canonization of Clare, taken in Assisi after her death. Amongst these devout women there must have been much talk of Francis, and, with some girl companion, Clare, already a leader in piety, would seek him out to talk with him; and he, having already heard of her notable virtues, gladly welcomed her. 'Many times,' said Madonna Bonna de Guelfuccio, 'I went with her to speak with St Francis, and went secretly for fear of her kin, and he taught her that she should turn to God.' Then her parents decided she should marry – some feudal union of lands – for she was 'fair of face'. But Clare's mind was fixed now on poverty. She appealed to Francis: once admitted to his Order, dedicated to the Church, she could face her father as he had once faced his. The bishop perhaps knew of it, for on Palm Sunday, the day before her flight, he signalled out Clare in the cathedral and with his own hands gave a palm to her. That night the doors were locked, the windows barred, but in these old Assisian houses there was a custom that one special door was kept – the door of the dead – through which a coffin passed and which was then blocked up again with stone and rubble: it was through such a door, perhaps recently used and easily cleared, that Clare escaped, and she was indeed dying to the old life of the world.

Her family at once sought her out and demanded her return; but she showed them her shorn head, and already there was something masterful and determined in this girl, before which people stood aside and let her have her way. The real struggle came some days after: Clare's younger sister, Agnes, escaped to join her. This time her uncle, Monaldo, the head of all the family, came with arms and force to bring back this second rebel. Agnes was dragged from the church, but, as they tried to carry her off, Clare came out undaun/ted, and, before her words and courage, once more their hearts failed them and they let Agnes go. *(Pl. IX)*

Already, then, there were two ladies in the Franciscan Order. Francis obtained for them the use of the Chapel of San Damiano, the beloved chapel of his vocation, and of the little house beside it. Here other ladies came and joined themselves to Clare: Pacifica, her mother's companion on pilgrimage; young girls she knew in Assisi or Perugia; Beatrice, another sister; the lady Ortolana herself. They lived on alms which the brothers begged for them, sewing and spinning, working in their little garden, taking in sick people to tend them. Francis characteristically thought little of the problems which this second Order had created; only when, in 1215, the Lateran Council prepared to legislate against new foundations, he persuaded Clare to become recognized as Abbess of the 'Poor Ladies,' strengthening thereby the monastic nature of their cloister. Clare, for her part, obtained from Innocent a privilege of Poverty, a title/deed to their way of life: and Innocent, saying that the demand for a title/deed to have nothing was a rare matter, wrote it for her with his own hand. For Clare this must have been something of a compromise. It had always been open to her to seek the monastic life in one of the established orders, and, if the family might have been reluctant to lose a marriageable daughter, there would have been no prolonged opposition to her vocation. With her force and energy of character, she must have hoped with Francis to be more active in the world, to share some of the duties of the friars. If so, it was a hope beyond her time. The *Fioretti* has a charming story of how Clare longed to share a meal with Francis, and begged that he would come and eat with her at San Damiano, but instead Francis sent some of the friars to bring her down to the Porziuncola, saying 'she has been a long while enclosed in San Damiano and it will please her to see again the friary of St Mary, since it was there that her hair was shorn and she became the bride of Christ.' While they met the whole chapel gleamed with light, and the people of Assisi hastened down thinking it was on fire. *(Pl. X)* Legend possibly, but a legend that seemed fitting to those who kept the tradition of the early days, and this happy unawareness of ecclesiastical conventions is very characteristic of the saint. But the official view was that Clare, till her death forty-one years later, never left San Damiano, though her influence steadily extended from the small, roughly built church and cloister. 'Ladies,' Francis liked to call them, not 'sisters,' for 'ladies' had the favourite ring of chivalrous parlance; but of Clare he always spoke simply as 'Christiana' – the Christian.

It was in Rome, on a visit about this time, that he met Jacopa of Settesoli, a widow lady of the house of Frangipani, administrator for her young children of considerable estates and engaged in much litigation over them – busy about many things. These feudal holdings were not hers to abandon. She had obligations enough to fulfil; and yet she was much drawn to Francis and his teaching. She could never be perhaps of the inner circle, of the few who had given

PLATE IX

ST CLARE SHOWING HER SHORN HEAD

'*Now when the report of these doings reached the ears of her kinsfolk, they passionately and bitterly condemned the maid's decision, and, in an angry body, hastened to the place where she was . . . urging her with threats of violence or with the poison of good advice . . . to leave so low and vile a life, unsuited to one of noble stock . . . But she, steadfastly resisting, laid hold of the altar cloths, and bared her shorn head, saying that nothing would now separate her from the service of Christ.' (Legenda S. Clarae C.V)*

15-25

their lives as examples to lighten the world, as Francis and as Clare had done: but Francis had no question of her sincerity of purpose. In his letter to all Christian people he writes of the life of penitence and alms-giving and abstinence lived in the world, and of 'the men and women' to whom he wrote Jacopa was doubtless one. 'Brother Jacopa' he nicknamed her; and this Roman lady, who ended her litigation when she came under the saint's influence, was thereby made an honorary member of his Order. He gave a lamb to her once, and, to please her, would eat the almond cakes she made so well; and in the end she watched over his deathbed. *(Pl. XI)*

CHAPTER SIX

MEANWHILE the friars had been busied in journeys about Italy. There was a group of them settled at Florence; the most experienced of their missionaries, Bernard of Quintavalle, had preached with such success in Bologna that he had begged Francis to send some other there, for he had too much honour in the place, and this after at first being received with derision in that learned city. Here and there, on the outskirts of towns, or in some quiet hill retreat, there were now small bands of the brethren scattered throughout central Italy. Once a year they would collect together at the Porziuncola, and Francis would speak to them, exhorting them to remain loyal to Poverty; reminding them, too, how in their journeys they must show all care and reverence to churches, or to wayside shrines, repairing them where needful, and always honouring all priests they met. But above all they must keep themselves from the entanglement of property. Francis, resting on one of his journeys, moved from a little hut they had made him only because one of the brothers referred to it as his; always again and again he was saying, 'The foxes have holes, and the birds of the air have nests, but the Son of Man hath not where to lay His head'; and he would share in that suffering and loneliness of his exemplar.

Then came wider plans. The visit of John of Brienne, King of Jerusalem, to Rome and France stirred once more crusading fervour. Kings and great nobles might be too busied defending their lands or adding to them, defining boundaries within which their interests were contained, and little ready for Eastern adventures; but among the ignorant and foolish there was still a yearning after Jerusalem. In June of 1212, in Vendôme, a shepherd-boy preached a crusade to his companions, and led them down to Marseilles, saying that the sepulchre would be freed by children. Francis may well have heard tell of it, or it may have been a moment when everywhere men's hearts, without conscious sense of a common reason, were feeling this old impulse; some time in that autumn of 1212 he set out for Syria. 'He was aflame,' says Celano, 'with the utmost desire for martyrdom, and determined to pass over to Syria to preach the Christian faith and repentance to the Saracens.' Thus simply was a great epoch of Christian missions reopened: simply and not very explicitly. Francis, when, after much endeavour he reached the infidel, seems

PLATE X

ST FRANCIS AND ST CLARE EAT TOGETHER

St Clare begged Francis that she might eat a meal with him, and when the brothers urged him to grant this request he said 'as it seems to you, so it seems to me. But that she may be the more consoled by it I wish that we eat together at S. Maria degli Angeli, seeing that she has been long enclosed at S. Damiano, so that it will rejoice her to come here, where her hair was shorn and she became the bride of Christ.' Clare came, and while she and Francis spoke together, the whole friary and the wood round about seemed ablaze with light, so that all the townspeople ran down to extinguish the fire, only to find that this was no earthly light. (Fioretti C.14)

Here, as in several of the drawings, St Francis has a double profile, one gazing at the luminous face of St Clare, one looking down at the head of one of the citizens.

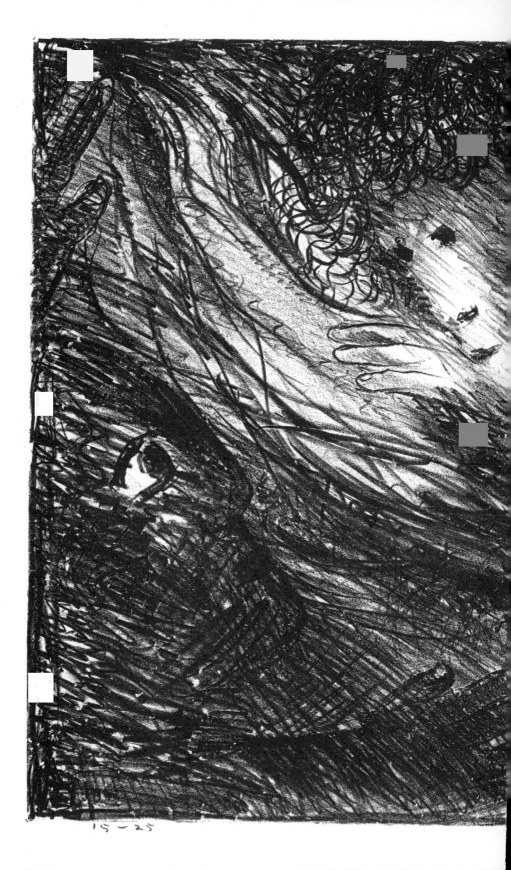

15 - 25

to have shown them the same courtesy, the same urgency of love with
which he won souls in Umbria; and the example of his method was
to be very fruitful, so that soon there were to be schools to train men
in oriental languages that they might speak to the heathen in their
own tongue. A hundred years after Francis's death there were fifty
Franciscan convents in and round Pekin. It was a development made
possible by amazing energy and devotion, and it was Francis that
inspired it; but its early growth was through this hectic craving for
martyrdom rather than any realization of common brotherhood.
When Giles and some other friars travelled to Tunis, the native
Christians there bade them be gone and not exasperate the Moors
against them all, and elsewhere in Morocco five of the brothers were
to bring death upon themselves through the outrageous abuses they
openly proclaimed against Islam. It was the fury of the early martyrs,
demanding their deaths and seeking to increase the torments – an
ecstasy, abnormal, repellent, and triumphant. It is in terms of it that
Francis's own conduct is described—'With all his might,' writes
Bonaventura, 'he sought death for His sake'—and in the romance and
adventure and selflessness he had full share, but not in its intem-
perance and violence and lovelessness. It was Brother Giles, the
the same who had boasted his faith so carelessly in Tunis, who in old
age was to say that he knew now that martyrdom was an easy matter,
and that the inner life of prayer was harder proof of man's constancy.
And it was with something of the same understanding that Bonaventura wrote of Francis that he was not given to testify to his Lord
with his life, but yet – thinking of the miracle of La Verna – the
Lord was to set His sign upon him, 'his flesh albeit not stricken by
the tyrant's steel, was nevertheless not left without the likeness of the
Lamb that was slain.' As yet, however, the attempted mission failed.
When Francis embarked with a few companions at Ancona, the
winds were unfavourable, and he was forced back on the Dalmatian
coast, where he could hardly find a boat to take him back to Italy,
though on the crossing he won the hearts of all the sailors in it.

Tired, and even his alacrity was not always proof against disappointment, Francis went to a small island on Lake Trasimene,

that lovely stretch of waters whose surrounding hills had all now
memories of his missions. Then in spring he was once more in the
Romagna, and it was in his preaching there one day, when, as often,
he took the refrain of a troubadour ballad, 'The joy I look for is so
great, 'Tis no labour then to wait,' that a certain noble heard him –
Orlando dei Cattani, Count of Chiusi – and asked him, if ever he
wished for a quiet retreat, to go to the lonely mountain of La
Verna, which from now on he would set aside for the brethren.
Peace and solitude and prayer – the thoughts matched with Francis's
inclination. There are in the legends hints of crisis in his thoughts:
once he had doubted even of his whole mission; whether this
hardship of life, this body-consuming fervour of example, was truly
God's will – and he thought, as every man must think, of wife and
family. Celano delights a little in these temptations; it is he who tells
us most of them, and decorates them with various scourgings and
mortifications, self-inflicted, or imposed in indignant frustration by
the Devil. But the Franciscan traits shine out from the conventional.
When such thoughts seized Francis, he stole out from the mountain
hermitage where he was resting. It was winter, and there was snow
in the Apennines: Francis made a snow woman and snow children,
and a late-waking brother heard him speak to them: 'Here is thy
wife and children: make haste and clothe them all: if, however, such
manifold cares trouble thee too much, leave them and serve God
only.' It was the restatement of his early conviction, that his work
could admit of no division, no compromise of affections. But in this
time of uneasy thoughts he longed for secluded contemplation, and
perhaps shrank a little from the problems of administration with
which the growth of the Order faced him. Back at the Porziuncola,
he unburdened himself to Brother Masseo, the sensible and clear-
headed, but he wanted more than human counsel. Masseo agreed to
lay the matter, with the impersonality of a second party, before
Brother Sylvester in retreat at the Carceri – a man whose spiritual
insight Francis trusted, knowing through what a contest he had
passed – and before Clare at San Damiano, already regarded as a
repository of prayer for the Order. From both the answer was very

definite: that Francis's vocation was to preach in the world; that it was given him not to save himself alone, but to save others. 'Then let us go forth in the name of the Lord,' said Francis, with complete and, it seems, permanent reliance on his decision; and with Masseo and knightly Angelo he set out on a new journey, once more through Ancona and the Marches.

It was on this setting⁄out that happened the best⁄loved incident of the Franciscan story – the preaching to the birds. By the wayside at Bevagna, some four hours' walk from Assisi, birds were gathered round some harvest⁄sowing, birds such as Italy had then, before 'the chase' had depopulated the countryside of its *ucceletti* – for now the birds of Italy have only rare sanctuaries, as in the woods round the Franciscan Carceri, where his memory still protects them. Francis could say hard things of 'brother body', and visit austerities upon it: he knew his career was only possible under the strictest discipline. But his asceticism held in it no contempt of the world, its practice was but to release a fuller joy in living: the lonely hillside was not only a hermit retreat, free from distraction, but in itself an inspiration. He was a true romantic, idealizing daily life and the incidents of it, and so a great nature⁄lover. Here, as so often, Francis breaks through contemporary limitation, and, defying history, relates himself most intimately to our own thoughts. And, as bird⁄lovers sometimes have, he had the gift of not frightening them. They came to him: and timid beasts too – rabbits, such as those El Greco was to paint him with, skipping in front of the grinning skull that the gloomy religion of Spain was to think more suitable for his meditation. 'My brother birds,' he said when he saw them, 'you ought always to praise and love your Creator, who has given you feathers for clothing, wings for flight, and all that you have need of. He has given you a dwelling in the purity of the air, though you sow not, neither do you reap.' It was a spontaneous babbling of the spirit, and the Christian imagina⁄tion has been much the richer for it.

There is another legend that deals with Francis's power over wild creatures, one that Celano and Bonaventura, if they knew of it, left out of their biographies, but which has none the less had wide and popular appeal. The town of Gubbio was much troubled by a fierce wolf that made inroads on their flocks and had killed some men. There were still packs of wolves in the Apennines, and this was no unusual menace. Francis 'felt great compassion for the people of the place', and alone, for none dared accompany him, made his way to the wolf's lair. He returned with the wolf meekly following him, and he persuaded the townsfolk to feed it; and for two years till it died the wolf was kept in Gubbio, a very peaceful and much regarded member of the city. Sassetta showed Francis, with the paw of the wolf in his hand, at the gate of the town, while a notary drew up a treaty with the beast. It is a scene of fantasy and charm, and shows what the fifteenth century sought for in the Franciscan legend. To Arthur Boyd the wolf is a terrifying, overpowering monster, a struggle between bestial and spiritual forces, a savage combat that looks back to earlier, more primitive forces. There is no better example of the continued potency and richness of the Francis-can myth. Some writers have sought to explain how the wolf was in fact a robber baron, called by Francis to repentance, but this only obscures deeper, more powerful meanings. The people of Gubbio

PLATE XI

THE GIFT OF THE LAMB

'*He once had with him in Rome, a lamb, by reason of his reverence for that Lamb most gentle, and he gave it to a most noble lady, one Jacopa of Settesoli, to be cared for in her house.*' Bonaventura *goes on to tell how the lamb accom-panied Jacopa to church, and if she was late in rising butted her gently and roused her with his bleatings.* '*Wherefore the lamb, that had been a pupil of St Francis, became a teacher of devotion, and was much cherished by the lady.*' (Bonaventura, Legenda Maior, C.VIII)

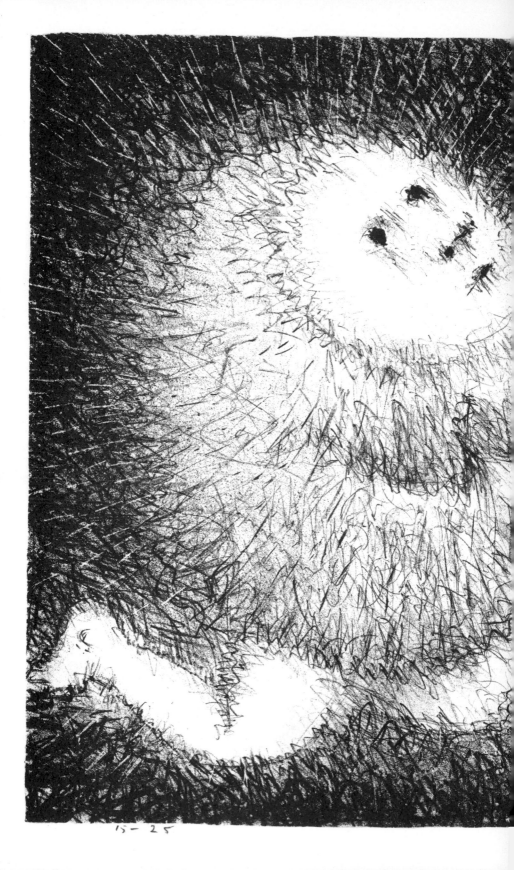

15-25

at least like to point to the fact that the skull of a very large wolf was found in the walls of the old church of San Francesco della Pace. *(Pl. XII)*

That winter – 1214 to 1215 – he went to Spain, drawn there, perhaps, because it too was a crusading country. He went by Languedoc, the land of heresies and troubadours, fell ill in northern Spain, and returned; and away from Umbria, where he was so watched and loved, we hear little of him, and only the bare outline of the journey, with all its new experiences, has been handed down to us. They were not very happy or successful, these early missionary journeys. The brothers, for the most part, knew no language but their own, and less of other peoples' customs. They were mistaken for heretics; they could show no authorization for their missions. Only here and there did they touch hearts and make converts. But there seems to have been no more hesitation with Francis now: in Italy the Order was growing with astonishing rapidity, and, more astonishing, with no novitiate, with admission in the hands of any of the brothers, there were few backslidings, very few dismissals. 'One became,' as Sabatier says, 'in a few hours a member of the brotherhood'; but if the time was short the test was searching. 'Sell all you have and give to the poor.' The wide response, under such stringency of condition, shows the deep uneasiness of the times in which Francis spoke. Men, too, of position were amongst those joining: Thomas of Celano, the chronicler and learned stylist, who was to be his official biographer; Elias of Assisi, or of Cortona, as he was often called though Assisian by origin, a man who from the trade of mattress-making had aspired first to teaching in Assisi and then had made some renown as a scholar in Bologna, a man of force, intelligence, and ambition, whose part in coming events was to be a very large one.

The summer of 1215 brought deep encouragement to Francis. In the autumn, Innocent III held in Rome his great assembly of the Church known as the Fourth Lateran Council. Amongst the agenda of discussion two subjects were of vital interest to Francis: regulations of new orders, and plans for a new crusading expedition eastward. Innocent preached at the opening: 'With desire I have desired to eat this Passover with you.' The pope knew that these moments were the climax of his career; that all his skilled legislation, his new patterns of organization, depended on his power to infuse the Church with something of his own ardour. He went on to talk of how they must purge the Church, expounding the ninth chapter of Ezekiel, where the righteous who mourn over iniquities are marked with the letter *Tau*, which prefigures in its shape the Cross. From then onwards Francis took these words to his heart, and the T, the mystic cruciform letter, became the sign of his Order: it stood now to him for the work of redemption, and for his own union in that work with the great powers of the Church militant. For, though his Order received no further definition from the conciliar decrees, it received confirmation. The council was agreed that the multiplica׳ tion of orders was a dissipation of the energies of the Church, and that the penitential confraternities were best employed as a reinvigora׳ ting element under the old rules of Benedictine monasticism or the Augustinian Canons, and it was on the latter model that Dominic Guzman, the able Spanish preacher to the Albigeois, then in Rome, was bade by Innocent to order his followers. But, in this tightening up of regulations, existing rules already confirmed were excepted, and the Franciscan rule specifically so. The curious medley of texts and generalized statements which Innocent had seen in 1210 remained *sui generis*: by its fruits it was known, for in Italy, if its wider future was yet uncertain, there could be no question but that Franciscanism was a factor of primary importance.

The crusading message was to be more slowly thought on; but one other gain Francis brought back from the council – his friend׳ ship with St Dominic. Over this meeting – the two founders of the two friar Orders coming into first contact at this great rep׳ resentative gathering of the Church – the imagination of later times has played freely. Friendship there undoubtedly was, and on Dominic's side something more – imitation; for it was from Francis that he learned the full value of poverty and something of the Fran׳ ciscan way to men's hearts; from now on his Order was to grow rapidly, and was soon to repay its debt to a Franciscan Order, which in its turn relied a little on Dominican example to smooth over awkward memories of its own founder's explicit injunctions. But for immediate needs the two saints had this in common – a noble missionary ideal. Dominic had striven with heresy in southern France, convinced that by persuasion only, not by force, could it ever be truly dealt with; and in this he was at one with Francis's passionate desire to teach and persuade the infidel. How often they met again is not certain: once in Rome, when they discussed the futures of their Orders with Ugolino, and both were resolute that their brothers should not receive preferment in the Church, nor friars become bishops and cardinals; perhaps yet another time when Dominic visited a chapter at the Porziuncola, and saw a gathering of the Franciscan Order in its homeland.

Within a year of the council, in July 1216, Innocent III died at Perugia, and in the instant intrigue for a successor the great man's body lay unguarded, and was robbed of its jewels in the night, a striking homily on the vanity of earthly riches. Francis was in Perugia at the time, and had been present at the great pope's death-bed, more loyally than many whom Innocent had trusted longer. Of the scenes at Perugia we have a first-hand account in the letters of James of Vitry, a canon of Namur, Bishop-elect of Acre, who had come to Perugia on his eastward crusading, and arrived to find all confusion, and Innocent dead that morning. He writes with skilled observation, and it is fortunate that now, and later in the East, he met St Francis. James was well acquainted with the piety of northern Europe; he had been a follower of Marie d'Oignies, a holy lady of Brabant, who had abandoned riches in something of Francis's spirit, though with none of his originality of method; and he was eager to find similar saintliness in Italy. But the Curia was a bitter disappointment to him. 'Hardly,' he writes, 'is any talk allowed of spiritual matters. One solace, however, I have found in these parts: many of both sexes, even wealthy and worldly, have left all for Christ and fled the world, who call themselves Brothers Minor, and who are held in great reverence by the pope and cardinals. They occupy themselves no way about temporal matters, but with fervent desire and vehement zeal they labour daily to withdraw souls that perish from the vanities of the world. . . . The women also live in hospices by the cities, receiving nothing, but living by the labour of their hands. But they grieve much that they are honoured more than they wish by clergy and laity alike.' It is the golden age: the friars and Poor Ladies still working with their hands, shunning all honours, unperplexed and happy.

To Innocent succeeded Honorius III. He was an old man, a little failing, but of good repute for holiness. 'Very simple and of much good will,' says James of Vitry, 'and had given almost all his goods to the poor' – a man, that is, very ready to appreciate Francis, and almost too ready to protect his followers. For from now on the relationship between pope and Order grew ever closer. And that growth in nearness was presided over and strengthened by Ugolino, Cardinal Bishop of Ostia.

He was at this time a man of some fifty years old, born of a noble family of Anagni, that town which produced so many prelates: he was trained in the law and deeply interested in it, but he was a man of wide culture also – musical, eloquent, vigorous, correct in all his activities. In 1216 the Cardinal of Sta Sabina, the first protector of the Franciscans, had died, and from then on Ugolino seems to have made the Order his especial interest, seeing in it great potentialities, and aware also of the grave dangers besetting it.

In the autumn of 1217 he met Francis in Florence, as the saint, with Brother Pacifico, the ex-*jongleur*, was setting out on a mission to France, in much excitement at visiting the land of his predilections, the land where 'the Sacrament was so highly honoured' (James of Vitry perhaps had told him of the great reverence for *Corpus Domini* in the pietistic north), the land of romance whose borders he had only touched on travelling two years earlier to Spain. But Ugolino was alarmed at the prospect of Francis's absence. He had schemes of his own in mind for the Order, and he needed Francis's aid in them: his departure now would be most impolitic, a word new to the Franciscan vocabulary and little likely to be understood by its founder. 'My lord,' said Francis, 'much shame will it be to me if, having sent my brethren into far countries, I myself remain in these parts and do not share in the troubles which await them.' The voice is that of Roland or Lancelot exalting the burden of unremitting example. At last, however, Ugolino obtained from him that he would stay in Italy: Pacifico went on alone, to return only in his master's last days. From now on the relationship between Francis and the cardinal was of the closest nature. They did not always agree; Ugolino wished for constant cooperation with existing institutions; he would have drafted friars into the higher offices of the Church and established the Order on a secure foundation of papal privileges. To him Francis was a prophet, not a man of affairs: that was the function of the Cardinal Protector of the Order. Ugolino had, moreover, good reason for fearing some jealousy of Francis in the Curia; for in the early months of Honorius's pontificate the pope had granted an unheardof privilege to the Franciscan Order, the Indulgence of the Porziuncola. Francis had once said that he would have no privilege from Rome except the privilege to have no privilege; but this was a privilege, not for the Order, but for all the poor people of Umbria, of Italy, of the world perhaps, friars or lay alike, and it was laid up in heaven, not on earth.

The history of the crusades is closely bound up with the papal assurance, given to all who took part in them in a spirit of true penitence, that the penalties demanded by divine justice – that justice which the penitent by his contrition accepted – should be remitted for all sins already done and confessed. This crusading indulgence was in its early days unique; though gradually, for other good works – particularly pilgimage, with its 'labour of journeying' – similar grants were given; and the visits of churches with donations for their repairs became a subject of temporary indulgence where needful. To Francis the idea of indulgence must have been much in mind while his thoughts were so full of crusading business; and his own restoration of churches suggested a nearer connection. He became desirous of obtaining this great privilege for those who could not go crusading, or make long journeys, or pay costly gifts. 'Holy Father,' he said to Honorius, 'but a little while past I restored for you a church in honour of the Virgin Mother of Christ, and I beseech your holiness that you bestow upon it an indulgence without oblation.' Without oblation, for what oblation can those who have nothing make? 'If it please your holiness, I would that whosoever should come to this church, confessed and contrite and absolved by a priest, should be freed from all guilt and penalty both in heaven and on earth from the day of their baptism till the hour in which they enter this church.' It was an unheard-of request. The cardinals cried out that it would render crusading indulgences valueless in the eyes of the people. But Honorius withstood them, and Francis was given the indulgence he sought, to be obtained every 2nd of August – the day, that is, which was now fixed for the consecration of the restored Porziuncola. He went away, without any formal grant made out. 'Simpleton,' said the pope, 'what proof will you have that this indulgence has been granted?' 'Your word, Holy Father,' said Francis; 'if it is the work of God it

PLATE XII

THE WOLF OF GUBBIO

Of all the tales in the 'Fioretti', the Wolf of Gubbio is the most popular. '"Brother Wolf," said the saint, "come here; I command you in the name of Christ that you do no ill to me nor to anyone."' And the said wolf lived for two years in Gubbio and went in and out of the houses as a tame beast, and was fed kindly by the people and no dog barked at him. (Fioretti C.20)

In Arthur Boyd's drawing, the wolf is a shaggy, menacing mass lying over the crouching Francis: the miracle of taming him has not yet happened, but already there is a symbol of that union with the animal world that was one of the saint's great attributes.

15 -25

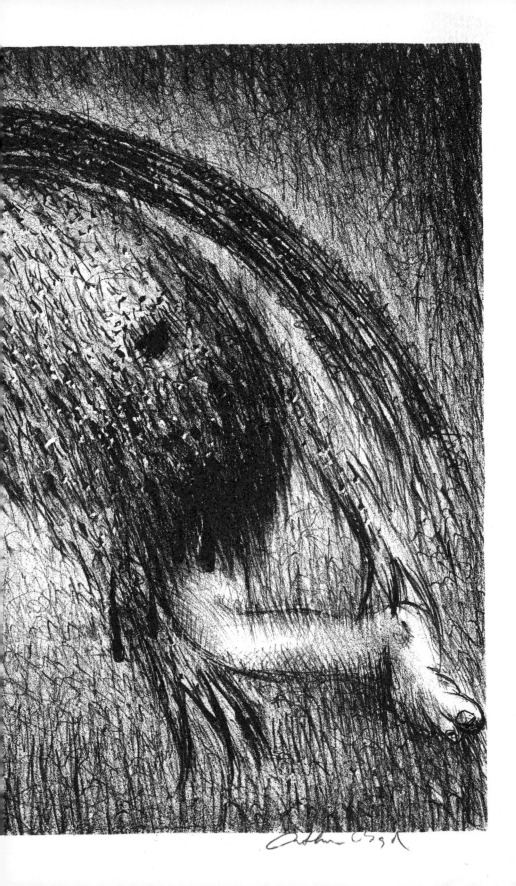

will be made manifest.' Francis preached at the consecration. 'I want,' he said, 'to send you all to Paradise, and I have received for you an indulgence from the lips of the Holy Father. And all you who have come here today, and all who shall come yearly on this day, shall have an indulgence for all their sins. I wanted it,' he added naïvely, 'for eight days, but I could only get it for one.'

CHAPTER SEVEN

THE attempted journey to France had been the outcome of measures taken in the summer chapter at Assisi. Such gatherings now numbered hundreds, perhaps thousands. It is most unlikely that anyone knew how many had been admitted to the Order, or that any kind of records had been kept. Now inevitably some systematization was required. Italy was divided into seven provinces, and over each was set a provincial minister. It was the first inroad on the primitive fraternal simplicity, where hitherto, in journeys or hermitage settlement, one would be chosen as 'Vicar of Jesus Christ' to direct the others, and they would all owe obedience to him 'as to a mother' who tended them. Francis, in this new appointment of provincial ministers, pleaded for the continuation of this tradition; they were to be ministers indeed, ministering unto the brothers and caring for them as a shepherd cares for his sheep. Ministers were also named for parts abroad – Spain, Portugal, France, Germany, Hungary, Syria – but, alas! the high hopes of these journeys were disappointed: north of the Alps the brothers could not make themselves understood, were taken for heretics, mocked, beaten, driven out, and returned disconsolate to Assisi. Only in Spain, under Bernard of Quintavalle's experienced guidance, did they have some success, and in Syria, where Brother Elias showed proof of exceptional skill and force. Yet the Order grew: in Italy its fame was great, and, despite the failure of the missions, members came from other countries. At the chapter of 1219 there are said to have been 5,000 present. The people of Assisi, proud and impressed at such gatherings, hastily put up a stone building by the chapel of the Porziuncola to provide some better meeting place. Francis, away at the time, was bitterly indignant when he returned and found it. What had they to do with stone buildings? With some of the friars he climbed the roof and began to pull it down, and only strong representations that it belonged to the commune persuaded him that he must not destroy it. But it was an eyesore in the sacred woodland of poverty.

Ugolino came to preside over the meeting, and his presence gave encouragement and opportunity to the voicing of views with which Francis could hardly be in sympathy. Some of the brothers went to the cardinal and asked whether more elaboration of the Rule would not be advisable for the ordering of so large a society. Francis had refused even to permit of provision being made for feeding such a multitude, though the charity of central Italy had justified him in this; he knew now that there were hesitations, and he made a vehement appeal to the chapter, with all his old ardour but with an undertone of bitterness not there before. 'My brothers, my brothers, the Lord called me by the way of simplicity and humility, and showed me that this was the true way for myself and for those who would trust in me and imitate me. And therefore I will that you name to me no other Rule, neither of St Benedict, nor of St Augustine, nor of St Bernard, nor any way and form of life other than that which has been most mercifully given to me by God. And the Lord said to me that He wished me to be a fool in this world . . . but you by your learning and wisdom He will confound, and I trust in the sergeants of the Lord, that through them He will punish you, and at length, will ye it or no, you will return with shame to your true estate.' By 'the sergeants of God' Francis meant the demons, the evil forces ready to possess the soul with temptation as soon as the unguarded moment came, and to punish the mind with despair and the body with sickness: and in the afterlife to be executants of the divine justice. Evil they are, for they exist through sin, but they bring also afflictions to curb sin, and as such they are God's servants; for under an omnipotent God the Devil himself may be agent for good. So far stood Francis from the debasing dualism of the Albigensians. When Ugolino and the friars heard this speech, and saw how clearly he faced the issue, they were afraid and said no more.

Beyond such disputes, Francis looked to the great crown of his design – new missions. As soon as the chapter was concluded, Giles departed to Tunis, and Francis himself, this time staying for no objections, to Egypt, to the crusading army gathered in the Nile delta at Damietta. In his place were left two vicars – Matthew of Narni and Gregory of Naples, a man of parts, eloquent and able, likely to dominate the simpler piety of his colleague. It was early June when Francis departed. On the 11th of that month Ugolino obtained from the pope commendatory letters that the brethren might carry with them as credentials on their journeys, and so avoid earlier missionary fiascos. Such letters were very necessary. Recently the Bishop of Paris had written to Rome asking what authority these wanderers had. Francis, however, had been bitterly opposed to them, and there is no record that he had agreed to their issue before his departure. To him they were without apostolic precedent, a diminution of the confidence that relied upon God alone. 'I tell you,' he exclaimed, 'by your humility you must first convert the prelates, and then they will call you to come and preach to their people.' But to Ugolino, with his wide view of Church reform, his pre-occupation with such matters as the planning of the Dominican Order, some measure of legalization seemed essential to the Franciscans, and he could not see the contradiction in the terms. A month after the papal letters he issued a new constitution for the Poor Ladies of Monticelli, where Clare's sister Agnes was abbess, of Siena, Perugia, and Lucca. San Damiano had its own recognition from Innocent, which Clare had so wisely obtained, and Francis had always claimed resolutely that her household there was a branch of his Order. With the others it was somewhat different: they were not directly under Clare, and already Ugolino as legate had had his part in their foundation. His new Rule was one of an exacting strictness in fasting, silence, and complete seclusion, an attempt to revive the severities of earlier times, and borrowing more from Citeaux than from Assisi. Clare herself practised an extreme discipline, as though cloistered poverty needed greater rigour than that lived in the world; but, like Francis, to others she always counselled moderation. Moreover, in Ugolino's Rule there was no mention at all of poverty. Its publication had an immediate effect. Brother Philip, one of the first twelve, whom Francis had left as special protector of San Damiano, who had accompanied him in his early interviews with Clare, urged her to accept the constitution. Those who desired, in the Order as a whole, approximation to older Rules saw in it an example to be followed; for that which they aimed at was not an easier life but stricter discipline; Franciscan freedom was too hard for them. Tentatively the vicars promulgated a code about fasting – that even on non-fast days the brothers should never seek for meat, though they might eat it if it were spontaneously given them; Monday was added to Wednesday and Saturday as a fast day. They seem perhaps trivial-ities, but it was the validity of their enforcement that mattered. Many brothers refused to obey them; and rapidly there was confusion in the Franciscan family. Some enthusiasts broke away into excess: John of Campello formed a band of lepers of both sexes, a pathetic parody of Francis's teaching, and sought approval for it from Rome. All the dangers that Ugolino had foreseen seemed suddenly pro-voked rather than prevented.

Meanwhile, in Morocco the Order was receiving its earliest martyrs. Five brothers had been grimly tortured and then executed, going with alacrity to their deaths, exasperating the Moorish authori-ties by preaching, to their profanation, even in the mosques. It was the very folly of fanaticism, and its crude aggressiveness lacks any true Franciscan beauty; but they died bravely after much torment, and some more timid Christians stole their bodies and carried them to Lisbon, for in death they had become relics, and of value. Francis, when he heard of it, was filled with deep joy that now he had indeed brothers in heaven. Blessed are they that are persecuted. Clare, worried with new problems in Assisi, had a moment of impatience, and longed that she too might seek missionary martyrdom.

Some time in July or early August, travelling with a few companions – Peter Catani, Illuminato, Leonard of Assisi – Francis had
reached the crusading camp at Damietta, where, dangerously placed
on both banks of the Nile mouth, an army had already been a year in
camp; and beyond them lay the Sultan of Egypt, El-Kamil, ready to
attack their position whenever they pressed hard the siege of the
town. An old friend was here, James of Vitry, Bishop of Acre, and
his letters, vivid and personal as ever, give a sad picture of the
demoralization of the camp, 'the pilgrims hastening from sin to sin,'
which must have been harshly disillusioning to the pious brothers
from Assisi. Soon after they had come there, on 29 August, the
Christian army attacked the Sultan's force, only to be tricked by a
feigned retreat and lured into confusion and heavy loss. There was a
tradition in the Order that Francis specially mourned over the
Spaniards, when he saw that their great impetuosity had left but
few of them; which can be well believed, for romantic courage
always meant much to him. In the camp his influence was soon felt;
many joined the Order, and were freely admitted in the open readiness of Francis's early way – rather too readily, James of Vitry
thought, who admired but also criticized: 'This Order increases
greatly through all the world, because it closely follows the way of the
early Church, yet there seems to us to be a danger in that not only the
perfect, but also the young and imperfect, who ought for a time to
have been restrained and tested under some monastic discipline, are
sent two by two throughout the world.' For Francis himself,
however, he had great respect and veneration: 'Their master, who
founded this Order, when he had come to our army, fired by the
zeal of faith crossed over to the army of the Saracens, and they
brought him before the Sultan, who for several days listened atten-
tively to his preaching, and then, fearing lest any of his army should
be won over to the faith of Christ, sent him back to us in all honour,
saying, "Pray for me, that God may deign to reveal to me that faith
which is most pleasing to Him." ' The picture is clear and in its
details convincing. El-Kamil was a mild and intelligent man, a
tolerant protector of the Christian minority in Egypt, the future

friend and correspondent of Frederick II. On the one side is the
eternal question of the cultured, cautious mind – 'What religion is
most pleasing to God?'; 'What is truth?' – on the other the enthusiasm of the unlettered, worn, passionate man, brought here in a
creative certainty of conviction, arrived through so many improbabil-
ities. 'Before he could come to the Sultan,' one of the brothers,
Jordan, tells of him, 'he endured much despiteful usage from the
soldiery, and, not knowing the language, amid the blows he cried
ever, "Soldan, Soldan," and so in the end was brought to him.'
With such detail later elaboration was not necessary, but to his
followers proved irresistible, and Bonaventura's life has a long dispute
with the Soldan's priests, a challenge to ordeal by fire, and other
pictorial matter of which more close contemporaries knew nothing.
(*Pl. XIII*).

PLATE XIII

THE ORDEAL BY FIRE

*In the 'Life' by Bonaventura there is an account of how, preaching before the
Soldan, St Francis offered to prove which was the surer faith, the law of
Mahomet or that of Christ, by entering a great fire along with the Soldan's
priests. The priests, however, on hearing this, fled from the Soldan's presence.
St Francis then offered to pass through the fire alone, but the Soldan, wonder-
ing at the saint's devotion, would not allow it.*

*This story, not found in any of the earlier texts, has little to commend its
probability, but the painters were drawn to it. Giotto in Santa Croce follows
Bonaventura closely: Francis stands by a burning pier, while the priests
hurry away. In Boyd's drawing there is more violence: an armed figure grasps
Francis, ready to plunge him in the flames. (Bonaventura, Legenda Maior
C.IX)*

On 5 November Damietta was captured, after a heroic defence of over a year. Within the walls a terrible sight met the crusaders. Plague had been added to the shortage of supplies: 'hardly were there,' says Bishop James, 'a hundred sound men in the town; and the dead lay about on the ground, for there were not enough living to bury them.' Among such scenes we know nothing of Francis's emotions: seldom was there more need for his compassion. But he was not for long in the victorious camp: some of the army began to disperse, and Francis found an opportunity of sailing for Palestine, the true land of his desire. He was there till midsummer, but we have no information as to his movements. It is likely that for a time he had some fever, for he returned to Italy a sick man, never fully to recover. This we know – that to Francis, with his keen imagination, there must have been moments of rare beauty in those lands of vivid recollection: Christmas, perhaps, in Bethlehem; Galilee in early spring. He did not at least attempt to return for the Whitsun chapter of 1220. Then a messenger came to him that the chapter had met in disorder; that the new constitutions were being issued, unacceptable to many of the brothers; that even now further privileges were being sought from Pope Honorius, and that the ladies of San Damiano had been deprived of their daughter houses and left in isolation. Francis was at his daily meal when the messenger reached him. It was a Monday – one of the new fast days – and they had meat on their table. Francis turned to Peter Catani. 'What shall we do, Dom Peter?' he said; for Peter was a learned man, and noble by birth, and Francis 'in his urbanity' always gave him this title; and Peter, in reverence for Francis, and perhaps as a jest between them, always gave it him back: 'Ah, Dom Francis, you must do as you please, for so you have the power.' 'Let us, then, according to the Gospel, eat that which is put before us.'

CHAPTER EIGHT

IN THE COURSE of August 1220 Francis reached Venice, returning
from the East. The crisis of his life-work was now upon him, and for
the next three years it is a different Francis, a tragic, passionately
determined figure – one, as Leo put it, 'not always able to keep from
vehemently grieving'. In the end he was to achieve a fuller peace,
but this was the time of striving: sometimes he was too tired to
retain his joyfulness. Yet he adhered steadily to the completeness of
his ideal. If their life of poverty owed its strength and virtue to true
imitation of Christ's practice, then compromise was an impossible
conception, and the demands of worldly wisdom, the suggestions of
common sense, were irrelevancies: once admit the least of them, and
all was lost, and the light was gone from the shining example of the
mirror of perfection.

Once landed in Italy, he went on to Bologna, the gate of the
Apennine passes, and a town of most disturbing rumour to him.
The Provincial of Lombardy was Brother Peter of Stacia, a learned
lawyer; and, in his eagerness for study, he had built a house for the
brethren in Bologna – no mere shelter, but a true convent, the
building of which had required considerable funds, and, directly or
indirectly, entailed the handling of money: it was a worthy rival of
the new Dominican school opened there the previous year, and
it was a complete infringement of Franciscan precept, for it was
thought of as their own property, and known as 'the House of the

Friars'. When Francis heard that phrase, 'he turned on his steps and went out of the city'. 'You seek,' he said to Peter of Stacia, 'the destruction of our Order': and all the friars were turned out of the dwelling, though some were sick and little able for such rigour. Francis himself was ill also: he had to ride now, mocking a little with his old humour at Brother Leonard, one-time mounted knight of Assisi, who walked beside him, and dispelling by his quick insight a rebellious thought in Leonard's mind.

Bologna revealed to Francis how far reports were true: already the news of his return was bringing comfort and enthusiasm to the loyal friars throughout Italy; but he did not make for Assisi; the Porziuncola as a scene for dispute must have been a bitter thought to him. The pope was at Orvieto, and Ugolino with him. The cardinal had undoubtedly supported the reformers: he himself had been responsible for the decree for the Clares: yet Francis clearly trusted him. Ugolino was outside the Order: he stood for the Church Universal, and rightly sought to find how the friars might best be used in its plans. Francis could see that, and he was always insistent on the honour due to the Church and its dignitaries; but he well knew that they might miss the true meaning of his brotherhood. It was all-important to talk with Ugolino, and there was that between them which made talk possible, a bond of real affection, if not perhaps of real understanding. At Francis's request the pope officially named the cardinal as Protector of the Order: its founder no longer felt his own authority enough.

In Orvieto, Francis came on still more activity of the dissentient brothers. There had been discussions as to the need for stricter ruling as to admissions: it was a question which the Order's rapid growth rendered essential, and here Ugolino obtained Francis's agreement to new legislation, though it must have been unwilling agreement, won from him only by the troubles of the time, for each new ruling meant a loss of the original spontaneity of that brotherhood who had found love and faith sufficient. A Bull was issued on 22 September by which a year's novitiate was declared necessary before anyone was admitted to the Order, and, after such admission, no one might leave it. No longer Francis, reading in men's souls, might recognize spiritual kinship with Brother Giles or Lady Clare at their earliest meeting. Too large now for personal control, the family became an institution.

A week later Francis was back in Assisi for an autumn chapter. With his return the powers of the two vicars had automatically lapsed. Now he determined, in the present stress, knowing himself to be a sick man, to set up a permanent minister-general over the Order, and for this he chose Peter Catani. There had been so much talk of discipline and regulation and organization: Francis doubted of himself whether he could steer so hard a course. The old buoyancy was gone. 'Now,' he said to the assembled brothers; and many wept, hearing him, 'on account of those infirmities, which Thou, O most sweet Lord, knowest of, being unable to have the care of the Order, I commend it to its ministers.' To some it seemed as though they were orphaned. Francis, however, had eased himself of the fret of administration, that he might take strength for a new battle, the preservation of his Rule. Something already had been achieved, for Ugolino had declared San Damiano exempt from his new decrees. That shrine of Franciscanism remained unaltered. Closing the chapter, Francis told them that he was remaining at the Porziuncola to meditate upon needful revisions in the regulations of the Order.

The original Rule, as we have seen, was largely scriptural. The hard sayings – 'Go sell all you have'; 'Take up your cross'; 'If any man come to Me, and hate not his father, and mother, and wife, and children, and brethren, and sisters, yes, and his own life also, he cannot be My disciple' – and the instructions to the disciples, 'Take nothing for your journey' – to these, the original inspiration and charter of the Order, were added some general regulations, probably given at the time of Innocent's confirmation of it. Anyone who came to the Order should be well received, and must sell all his goods, or at least forsake them; the brothers were to have no 'domin-ion amongst themselves', but each was to serve the other; all were to labour if they could, and support themselves by it as far as was possible; and, finally, a profession of faith that all the brethren were

Catholics, and would live and speak Catholically, and should hold all clerics and religious as their masters in matters pertaining to salvation. This was the draft on which Francis was working in the winter of 1220, aided by Cæsar of Speyer, the learned and enthusias￼tic friar whom he had first met in Syria and who had come back with him, and who, when troubles came after Francis's death, was to be the first martyr for the strict observance of this Rule, in the composition of which he was now helping.

To the original Rule various decrees were added, regulations that had probably been drawn up in chapter meetings as the work had expanded: the division into provinces, fasts and the saying of offices, and, in the forefront of all, the new papal decree about admission to the Order. Underneath much of the wording the battle is visible: the clergy may have books for their offices, laymen who can read may have a psalter (and even while Francis was at the Porziuncola, working on the Rule, he had been much vexed on this question); but there are to be no new fast days; indeed, apart from Advent and Lent, Friday is the only fast day named, whereas originally it would seem to have been Wednesday as well; and the brothers might eat of all food that was put before them, according to the Gospels: there are now ministers in the Order, a minister￼general and provincial ministers, but the ministers are to remember the meaning of their title and are to act as servants and no brother is bound to obey them 'against our way of life or his own conscience', and all the brothers must guard against irritation and anger at the sins of any of their brethren, 'lest the Devil by the fault of one corrupt many.' Money must be scrupulously avoided, and no true brother will even touch it, though in the 'manifest necessity of the lepers' it may be accepted in alms – a piece of inconsistency typical of the haphazard growth of the Rule, and typical also of the problems which Francis had to face in his great quest for exact imitation.

About women there was a clause reflecting recent doubts and Ugolino's intervention, but reflecting also Francis's thought on the subject: no friar must henceforth receive any woman to the obe￼dience of the Order. Those early days of Clare's coming to the

Porziuncola are past, and in the great Franciscan expansion no longer possible: such methods in this numerous body, with so little means of supervision, might well lead to sad scandal. 'All brothers,' the clause goes on, 'must guard themselves against evil gazing upon women and frequenting with them' – 'A malo visu'; the phrase is vague, but the reference clear enough, and illustrated in the concluding words: 'And we must all keep watch upon ourselves and keep our members in all purity, since the Lord says, "Whosoever looketh on a woman to lust after her, hath committed adultery with her already in his heart." ' Clean and untroubled thoughts – this, as ever, remains Francis's teaching, and he would have been content to trust them with less trammelling. The clauses dealing with preaching and missions also bear the mark of recent experiences: brothers may not preach without the authority of their provincial minister, and this must be cautiously given; but there is no word of papal letters of recommendation or of other authorizing; instead, Francis breaks out in a great exhortation that none should glory in the success of their own preaching, for it is the Spirit that worketh with them; if they seek learning and forethought that they may speak eloquently, then that eloquence is their reward, but if they think not of their own words, but of the effect of the preaching and of their unworthiness to be God's instruments, then they will be seeking for true wisdom, for 'godly fear and godly love'.

Then follows advice about confession and the receiving of the sacrament. At the Lateran Council in 1215, Francis had heard Innocent's new confessional legislation and his definition of the meaning of the change in the elements. These thoughts were now constantly with him, and were more and more recurrent in his teaching. In the tradition of sacramental grace his experience is one of the most complete and notable testimonies. For him the Eucharist is the great centre of the Christian faith, in which heaven and earth are at one, and reconciled to omnipotent God. The corporal showing forth of the Spirit, the recurrent miracle of incarnation – this, by whatever symbols we think of it, is the essential Christian inspiration: in no other faith is there this promise that God, transcendent and absolute, has fusion with the finite and mortal; that the divine ever seeks to enter the human. 'Daily,' wrote Francis, 'He humbles Himself as when He came from the heavenly seats to the Virgin's womb; daily He comes to us, humbly appearing; daily He descends from the bosom of the Father, upon the altar, in the hands of the priest.' It was to this that Francis's deepening religious powers were steadily leading him: God has given us a real sense of His presence – 'Because except in this I see nothing corporally of the most high Son of God' – and 'presence,' the unspoken communica‑ tion between man and man, the perception of nature, meant wonderfully much to Francis. God has given Himself for us, and continues to do so, and enables us to share in the sacrifice, for in this most holy mystery man identifies himself with God. To Francis, happily unaware of the bitterness of later controversy, the receiving of the Body and Blood of Christ was the great Christian privilege and obligation: and the priests who administered it were worthy of all reverence – 'I am unwilling to consider any sin in them, since

PLATE XIV

ST FRANCIS CLEANSING THE LEPER

In a lazar house tended by the friars there was one leper who abused everyone who served him, and blasphemed God saying 'What peace can I have from God, who has made me all rotten and stinking?' St Francis came to him and asked what he could do for him, and the leper said 'Wash me all over for I stink so strongly that I cannot endure myself.' 'Then St Francis forthwith had water heated with many sweet smelling herbs, and then stripped the leper, and began to wash him with his own hands, and another brother poured out the water. And by a divine miracle, at the touch of St Francis's holy hands, the leprosy departed and the flesh remained perfectly sound.' (Fioretti C.24)

15— 25

through them I discern the Son of God.' Francis may have affinities
with that unrest of his time, which in some places engendered
heresy, but he is fast grounded on the Christian faith; he has penetrated to the heart of its theology, and no outward, temporary
preoccupation can obscure the meaning of the Christian Church
for him. It is as a great Christian that St Francis matters to us. If
we think of him as the sweet poet of Umbria, or as the social
reformer of Assisi, we wrong his greater glory.

So in the course of the winter Francis meditated on the Rule, and
we have in Leo's *Mirror* many incidents of this time: how already
some brothers pressed Francis for readings on difficult points; how
once a provincial minister said to him: 'What shall I do, who have
so many books that they be worth more than fifty pounds?' and
Francis said to him, 'I neither will nor ought nor can go against my
conscience and the Perfection of the Holy Gospel which we have
professed'; and when the minister looked sad at this, Francis cried
'with great fervour' before the brothers there: 'You would be seen of
men as Friars Minor and called observers of the Holy Spirit,
but for your works you want store chests.' About this time a poor
woman came begging to the Porziuncola; she had given two sons to
the Order, and Francis was ever especially considerate of those whom
he called the mothers of the Order; but at the time the brothers
themselves had no alms – nothing they could give to meet her need –
so Francis took from the altar their only Testament and gave it her.
'It will please God more than for us to read in it.' So, while he had
resigned the headship of the Order, Francis remained its conscience:,
and was acutely aware of being so, inasmuch as while he worked
upon the Rule he looked more and more scrupulously upon his
own life and conduct. One day he found, in the church at the
Porziuncola, James, one of the brothers, whom they called the
Simple, who had brought with him a poor creature far gone in
leprosy. Francis rebuked him, saying, 'You should not bring the
Christians (so he always spoke of lepers) out of their hospitals';
but, after James and the leper had gone, he suddenly was afraid that
the leper, hearing him, had felt hurt and ashamed. Turning to

Peter Catani, he said: 'You must in no way contradict the penance I have chosen for myself' – for, now that Peter was minister-general, he always consulted him – and Francis brought back the leper, and, sitting with him, ate out of the same dish. Leo was there, and, when he writes of it, cannot forget the repulsion of it, for the leper's hands were especially affected, with matter oozing from them. They knew very little perhaps of hygiene, though their disregard of it was not always from ignorance, but they had marvellous control over the weakness of the flesh *(Pl. XIV)*.

To this period of work and devotion – anxious work, but done with faithful friends at the beloved home of the Order – there came a sad end. On 10 March 1221, Peter Catani died. With Bernard of Quintavalle, he had been the first to come to Francis; and since then few had been so constantly with him or so much relied upon; without him the completion of the Rule and its acceptance by the chapter became a different matter. It was probably following Peter's death that Francis went to Rome, taking the revised Rule with him. The new minister-general, appointed without waiting for the chapter, probably by Ugolino in his new position of protector, was Brother Elias. He had returned with Francis from the East, and his proved experience had been in Syria, far from the internal divisions of the Order, a strong man for whom Francis had much affection, the attraction of opposites, and Ugolino confidence. As yet he was associated with the stricter views, but also known at Rome as a sound negotiator. Immediately on his appoint-ment a new Bull was received (21 March) authorizing the Order to celebrate mass in their churches during the time of interdict – a special mark of papal favour, but an implied recognition of the fact that the Order would have churches of their own, a thing which Francis, when he rebuilt the edifices of Assisi, had never intended. It was significant enough of the direction in which Elias's policy was to develop.

It was significant, too, of some of the problems facing Francis in Rome. For he had found that Ugolino had received representations from various provincial ministers as to the impossibility of the full

Franciscan code: in particular protesting against the clause, 'Take nothing with you on the road.' Dominic was at the time in Rome, in consultation with Ugolino, and the modified, rationalized poverty of his Order, growing now very rapidly, must have influenced Ugolino's views; in the discussions over the form of the Rule, the clause 'Nihil tuleritis' – 'Take nothing with you' – was omitted. 'They think,' said Francis, 'to deceive God.' To him, perfection permitted of no diminution. It was grief indeed that that clause was wrest from him. He might safeguard what remained by the final clause, forbidding any subtraction or addition or alteration of the Rule, but already compromise had pierced to the heart of it.

In the discussions in Rome there had been a further question of another Rule. In his missionary journeys Francis had made many contacts with men and women whose hearts were stirred by his message, though they yet remained in the world. Francis regarded his Order as an apostolic institution, for evangelizing mankind by the power of its perfect imitation; but the Christian life, he well knew, could be lived under other conditions; property must be held, as La Verna itself belonged to Orlando of Chiusi, and many feudatories could not legally part with their life-interests in their lands, even if they would – Jacopa of Settesoli remained trustee for her children – but property must be administered as an obligation and responsibility, and it must always be remembered that poverty, that great 'disencumberer of the Spirit', was the true joy. Already, before the times of trouble, Francis had written a letter 'to all Christians': 'Let us have charity and humility and let us give alms; we must also fast and abstain from vices and sins and from super-fluity of food and drink; and be Catholics.' The old simple precepts: moderation and discipline, obedience to the Church and accep-tance of the sacraments as a great vehicle of grace.

Now, however, Ugolino desired that there should be further regulation, and, though we have no Rule till 1228 – after Francis's death – from now on Christians living under Francis's inspiration came to be known as the Order of Penitents, third in this hierarchy of friars, Poor Ladies, and laity, and hence later to be known as tertiaries. Such penitent bodies were not unfamiliar. Innocent III had legislated for such a one in giving a Rule to the Humiliati, and it was from this Rule that Ugolino borrowed many of his clauses, particularly that whereby the tertiaries were forbidden to take unnecessary oaths or bear arms, and thus were brought outside the feudal framework, not without profit to the civil as well as the spiritual power of the Church. This question of oath-taking, the need for it in ordinary medieval business, and the Gospel prohibition, 'Swear not at all,' was a heart-searching problem of the time, very like evangelical poverty. There are in the organizations of the Tertiary Order ingenuities removed from Franciscan guilelessness, but it is at the same time a great monument to Ugolino's far-seeing judgement. Without some such scheme much of Francis's influence might have been forgotten and lost. By this careful, if incongruous, planning, it found wide and ready preservation.

CHAPTER NINE

AT Pentecost the chapter met. Elias presided, and Francis sat below him, twitching his tunic when he would draw his attention, seeking his leave when he wished to speak. Francis preached at the opening on the text, 'Blessed be the Lord my God, who teacheth my hands to fight'; 'exhorting to strength, admonishing to patience and to the setting forth of an example to the world.' A great number of brothers had come together – 3,000 according to Jordan of Jano, who himself was there, and has left us an account of it as direct and fresh as anything in Franciscan literature. 'How great at that chapter was the love between the brothers, and patience and humility and obedience and good humour.' The main business of it was the Rule; though Jordan, looking back at it from more troubled times, says nothing of this: and, moreover, he was occupied enough with his own affairs, for at this chapter came his own crisis.

Of the missions sent out in 1219 none had failed so completely as that sent to Germany; for when they had entered Germany, and did not know the language, and were asked whether they wished lodging or food or such-like, they answered 'Ya,' and so were by some charitably received. And seeing that by this word 'Ya' they were kindly entreated, they decided that they should reply 'Ya' to everything that was asked them. When, therefore, it happened that they were asked whether they were heretics, and whether they had come to pervert Germany as they had perverted Lombardy, and they answered 'Ya,' some were imprisoned, and some stripped and led about naked and made ludicrous in the eyes of men. The brothers then, seeing that they could have no fruit in Germany, returned to Italy. Whence it was that Germany was held amongst the brothers as so brutal a place that none would dare to return there unless inspired by longing for martyrdom. Such a defeat and such timidity could not pass unnoticed by Francis. 'Why,' he said, 'the Germans are very pious folk, whom often we see passing through Italy with their long staves and their bottles going on pilgrimage to Rome.' He would not order any to return there, but to those that were willing to go he would give the same mission, yea, a greater one, than to those going beyond the sea. In reply to this appeal, ninety of the friars eagerly came forward, and Francis gave the charge of them to Cæsar of Speyer, the friend with whom he had been so closely working, and bade him choose a party from among them. Jordan gazed at the devoted band; he had been regretting that he had never known any of the brothers martyred in Morocco; he would not now miss another opportunity; he pressed forward and began to ask them their names, 'thinking it would be great glory if martyrdom were to come to them, and he could then say "that one I knew and that one." ' But alas for his unwariness! Cæsar was choosing his little band, saw Jordan amongst them, and bade him come with them. Jordan protested: he had sought only to know their names; but the others pressed him to come. Terrified at the thought of Germany, certain he could not endure suffering, feebly murmuring of his weak health, he yet felt conscience awakening. He hurried to a brother whom he knew, tried in many tribulations, for six times in Hungary he had lost all, even his breeches. 'Go to brother Elias,' said his counsellor, 'and do that which he orders, and so free yourself from this perplexity.' And so it was that Jordan, with Cæsar of Speyer, Thomas of Celano, Francis's chronicler, John of Plan Carpin, the great traveller, and others whose names were to be famous, went to Germany, to fare much better than Jordan had feared. And through his pious snobbery and his childish enthusiasm glints simple Franciscan honesty. It was of such that the Order was made.

The two years that followed the chapter of 1221 and the re-editing of the Rule were sad ones, in which Francis bore much suffering of mind and body. While in the Rule he had sought to maintain the inspiration of the Order in its purity, he could not but be aware that Elias and Ugolino both considered some compromise necessary; and, while there were triumphant moments, as when the German mission returned with happy news of success, there were grumblings and discontent within this family which he had built up on love and self-abnegation. Some of the loyal brothers came to him once and asked him whether they should not separate themselves from the Order – an ominous forecast of what might happen when Francis's personal ascendancy was gone. But to such Francis counselled always patience: 'He truly abides in perfect obedience who sustains persecution rather than wishes to be separated from the brethren, for he lays down his life for his brothers.' That there was a final obliga-tion to the individual conscience, Francis admitted; if the Rule were indeed abandoned, then blessed would be the few who, apart by themselves, still maintained it; but that could only be considered as the final calamity. Meanwhile, if it might be right to disobey certain commands, those who did so must accept the punishment for doing so, rather than regret the authority which enforced it. But, alas! how far were such punishings and such authority from Francis's own intention. When some of the zealous asked him to exert himself against the laxer brothers, he answered: 'Since I am not able to correct them by preaching, admonition, and example, I will not become as an executioner, punishing and flogging them, like the magistrates of this world.' To the 'Lord's Sergeants' he would leave dissentient friars; he himself would not punish them: 'Yet truly, until the day of my death I will not cease at once, by example and the good works which the Lord has shown me, to teach the brethren, and walk by the way which I have taught and shown them by word and example, that before God they may be inexcusable and I not accountable for them.'

This burden of example weighed heavily upon him. Was the fault in him that so many were going astray? In the very size and success of the Order was its danger: he no longer could exercize over them that personal influence which fervently and passionately he held to have been true and good. 'After the Lord multiplied the number of the friars, I handed over the Rule of the Order to the Lord and the ministers, and I excused myself in the chapter-general on the ground of my infirmities, but even now, if the friars wish to walk according to my will, I would not that they should have any other minister until the day of my death.' More and more strictly he searched his own life to see whether in it there were not perhaps some cause of stumbling; and with new demand for old conventions, fasting and so forth, those sometimes substitutes for humility of soul, Francis doubted of how some might interpret the intercourse between the brothers and the sisters of San Damiano. Before, he had never hesitated to go and visit them: now he abstained, for fear that in his going others should receive offence. Clare, however, refused such thoughts: ready as she was for all discipline, eager in performing the meanest task of her household, this new sacrifice she would not tolerate – this doubt, as it seemed, which Francis now had in his early inspiration – and in the end her clear enthusiasm won. Francis came again and visited the Ladies; but it was to be very seldom, and never perhaps quite as it had been.

But of questions openly in dispute, the most vexed was over places of learning. Dominic had died in Bologna in the summer of 1221, but already his Order had a house of study there, and was becoming renowned for it. Franciscan emulation had been stayed by Francis's unhesitating closure of the house secured by Peter of Stacia; learning meant books, and some settled place to read and ponder them in; it was work suited to the quiet of the cloister. To Ugolino it seemed essential that in this vast organization, called into being by Francis's sanctity, there should be some nucleus of informed, learned opinion. By the fiction that the house and books belonged to him, and that the friars only had the use of them, he persuaded Francis to allow the Bolognese house once more to be re-opened; but only unwillingly, and his fears frequently brought Francis to Bologna at this time. We have an account from an eye-witness of how one day he preached there, on his favourite theme of love and amity, and how, in this learned city, the words of this 'simple fellow; this ill-clad, ugly, inconspicuous, little man,' persuaded many of the noble families of the city to abandon their ancient feuds. But of the feuds within the Order abandonment was to be harder. Perhaps, however, it eased Francis's mind that there was found at this time among the brothers a great preacher and theologian, Antony of Padua; and if at first Francis sanctioned his teaching with a reminder that preaching came from prayer rather than learning, later he grew in confidence, and wrote to him as 'Brother Antony, my bishop' – or was it confidence, and not perhaps something ironical? He would never have written thus to Leo: it was a different term from the diminutive nicknames of the early band.

Francis's own personal attitude to learning was clear and straightforward enough. The conviction had grown on him that he and his friars were to be simple folk, and that, while others might well serve the Lord by learning, they were to do so by prayer and example: it was not their learning that was to convert men, but 'the prayers and tears of holy, poor, humble, and simple friars, themselves knowing nothing of it.' These were his true 'brethren of the Table Round'. 'Whoso would be a true Friar Minor must have nothing save only, as the Rule allows, a tunic and cord and breeches, and those who need them, shoes.' Thus he said to a novice who had received permission from Elias to have a breviary: worrying Francis for his permission also, the novice had wrung from him in a moment of impatience the remark, 'Act as your minister has told you': but then Francis had run after him and knelt before him, confessing that he had been at fault in admitting such an exception against the Rule.

In incidents such as this lay a fatal source of friction: to Elias as minister belonged the office of authority, but the sanction of reverence belonged to Francis. Given Elias's permission, a brother would still seek Francis's approval; and Francis, with his theory of obedience not necessarily implying assent, was by no means always ready to endorse the minister's actions. The problem pressed heavily on him: 'there is no perfect obedience,' he said, 'unless one is an inanimate

corpse'; and then characteristically added, as his fancy played with
the simile: 'which only looks down if raised up, and only seems paler
if put in purple.' Many in all sincerity felt the situation to be impossible. The Rule of 1221, purporting, as it did, to embody the
meaning of the original Rule, had not been officially approved by
the papacy: a demand now arose that it should be revised so that it
might be exactly enforced, and then given formal papal sanction, so
that even Francis himself could not question any of the modifications
made in it. And that it should contain some modifications was
undoubtedly intended.

Wearily Francis returned to the reediting of the Rule – that Rule
whose final clause had proclaimed its immutability. Taking with
him Leo and another brother, Bonnizzo, he withdrew to a rock
cave on Mount Rainerio, above Rieti, on the lands of a Lady
Colomba, who welcomed Francis there, leaving him in peace and
quiet. We know nothing of her, but she is another of these women's
names which make complete the Franciscan legend. The chief
problem of these new debates was that of discipline: how was the
ministergeneral to enforce his authority? From his retreat Francis
wrote to Elias, in all friendliness: 'If there be anywhere a brother who
sins, as much as anyone can sin, let him not depart from before your
eyes unforgiven, if he seeks forgiveness; and if he does not seek it,
you must ask of him if he would not have it; and if thousands of
times he has to seek forgiveness from you, yet you must love him
more than you love me, because he is one whom you are drawing to
God'; and again: 'if the brothers are a hindrance to you, you must
bear it gratefully, and love them for it, and wish them no other than
they are, for then they will become better Christians: and be this
more to you than any hermitage.' Francis is writing in passionate
dread lest his rule of love should become a cause of stumbling,
breaches of which were sins, and punished as though not only sins,
but also legal offences; and he is writing as to a man he loves, a man
capable of sharing his views, who longs for the hermitage by Cortona
which Elias had often frequented, to which in pique or in piety he
might again return. Elias, in his ambitions and his sense of power,

had his own heart-searchings. But the practical difficulties remained: the Order taught obedience and lacked means to enforce it. Francis had solved the difficulty for himself by asking Elias that one of the brothers should always act as 'a guardian' for him, to whom he should owe complete obedience. He now often did his charities, his severities, in secret, lest the guardian should stop him. And in his letter he talks of guardians, and seems to suggest some extension of the system of brothers taking charge of brothers in mutual service. But at best these are problems remote from the spirit: in the first Rule, Francis had written, 'Let no one be called prior': they might still avoid names of pre-eminence, but the facts were not hidden by any avoidance.

From Rieti Francis seems to have sent a draft of the revised Rule to Elias, and then to have gone to Assisi for the Whitsun chapter to discuss it. But when he was come there, Elias told him that he had lost the draft. It was, in fact, a refusal to accept it. To oppose Francis may well have cost him much; and it is fair to think that Elias did it because he believed that stricter rulings were necessary. Ugolino and many others who loved Francis undoubtedly supported him. When Francis retired once more to Fonte Colombo, the retreat at Rieti, to write the Rule yet again, perhaps not realizing fully what its 'loss' meant, a deputation followed him to make the position clear – that there must be real modification. It was the hardest moment of all, and Francis's passionate sorrow burst out in his talk with Leo: 'This is my great grief and affliction, that in those matters which I have had confided unto me by God in His mercy, in those matters some brothers from the authority of their knowledge and their false forethought are opposed to me, rendering them void and saying, "These things are to be observed, these not." ' In his own heart he had no doubt: the way had been divinely shown him; it was no subject to be modified by legislation: it was *his* Order, which he could authorize, because to him the revelation had come. That – and he never hid it – was his inmost thought; but he knew the dangers of it – dangers to himself, dangers to the Church: 'It would seem to me that I am no Friar Minor if I do not rejoice equally when the brothers reproach me and cast me out, unwilling that I should hold prelacy over them, as when they revere and honour me; for in either case the profit is equal. For when they exalt me, I rejoice on account of their profit; yet my soul may be in peril thereby. Much more ought I to be glad and merry for the profit and salvation of my soul when they scorn me, for then there is certain gain of my soul.' Their profit was in following him and his Rule, he had no doubt of that; but the contamination of his Rule might be a sacrifice deman-ded of him. After Elias and the deputation had gone, Francis went to Rome.

For a time he parted from Leo, and such a parting was hard then, but perhaps needful, for Francis had always feared lest there should be jealousy of his closer friends, and had wished even in friendship, which he held so dear, never to be grasping. Thinking of his own riches there, he had pointed once to a blind man, led by a puppy, as a reminder of what true poverty meant. But he now gave a letter to Leo, the original of which is still preserved, bidding him come to him whenever he desired: and this, too, he wrote in it: 'My son, as a mother to her child I answer "Yes." This word resumes all our talks by the wayside, and all my opinions. . . . Whatever be the way in which you think you can please God, to follow His footsteps and live in poverty, take it. God will bless you, and I authorize you to it.'

The new Rule as it was approved by Honorius III on 29 Novem-ber 1223 was a very altered document from the Rule of 1221. It was much shorter, much more relevant, much more a legal act. The passionate appeals, the admonitions which break through the earlier Rule, the Biblical quotations, the prayers, the individuality, are gone. In matter the changes are subtler, but important: procedure for the election of the minister-general is laid down; and where, before, the brothers could observe the Rule literally, even against the minister-general's interpretation, now his consent to their reading of it becomes necessary; the brothers are forbidden to enter 'the convents of nuns', a clause which later was held to include even San Damiano, though 'nuns' was not a term ever used by Francis of his Poor Ladies. There is no word of 'guardians', but, under the provincial minister, there is a new officer, the custodian – a different-sounding word; and where before there had been the words of the Gospel for the sending out of the disciples, the very crux of the whole Franciscan message, there is only a pathetic appeal from their founder that they should not 'quarrel, nor contend with words upon the way, nor judge one another, but that they should be peaceful; and that they ought not to ride, unless by manifest necessity.' But the omissions Francis regretted above all others were those clauses which had dealt with the blessed sacrament: he would indeed have added new ones, wishing his friars to teach a special reverence for it, and to see that it was kept with all seemliness, carrying with them 'fair and clean pyxes,' and even 'wafer irons for making fair and clean hosts.' Now there was no mention of the sacrament: it was thought such propaganda might cause trouble with parochial priests: it was not considered very necessary or relevant.

Through it all he remained most faithful to his own ideal: when he stayed with Ugolino and fed at his table, he would bring in fragments that he had begged as alms and feed on them; and when he stayed with Cardinal Leo Brancaleone, who gave him a tower in the garden wall for himself and Angelo Tancredi, that he might rest there, he doubted but that other brothers might say, 'He lives with my lord cardinal'; so, though he owned that 'it was very necessary for his body to receive rest', he returned to one of the mountain hermitages.

PLATE XV

JACOPA OF SETTESOLI AND THE DISH OF
MOSTACCIOLI

St Francis when he was dying recalled how in Rome the lady Jacopa had often made a sweetmeat for him, out of almonds and sugar and other things, which the Romans called mostaccioli, and he asked the friar to let her know that he was dying, so that if possible she might come to him. But before the letter was despatched, there was a knocking at the door, and Jacopa and her sons were without, bringing a shroud, wax for tapers, and a dish of the sweetmeat. (Speculum Perfectionis C.CXII)

CHAPTER TEN

WITH the journey to Rome and the authorization of the Rule the problems of organization seemed, for the time at least, to be settled. Now there was a minister and a defined code to direct him: for the Holy Man himself, for the fount of this new inspiration, there seemed a resting-space. Gladly Francis withdrew a little, from distractions which galled his spirit and in which his presence some/ times seemed an irritant. Still a sick man, his eyesight ever more impaired, he might refuse all comforts, mockingly turning outwards the fur they sewed inside his tunic against the winter cold, but rest brought some strength to him. Another friend in the Rieti lands, John of Vellita, had prepared for him a rock cell by the hill town of Greccio, cold enough quarters but sheltered by some woods. Here with a few companions Francis spent winter, and waited there for spring and Easter. And those who were with him long remembered how, for the Christmas Mass at Greccio, Francis had had a crib made and filled with hay, and brought some oxen to it, that the beasts too might bear their witness. 'I will make a memorial,' he said, 'of that Child who was born in Bethlehem, and in some sort behold with bodily eyes his infant hardships.' Ever the question of example, and the fine, naïve sense of dramatization. At the Mass he served as deacon, and preached also. Friars had come in from the surrounding neighbourhood, and, as always with Francis's preaching, it was the inward glow they remembered, not the substance of his meaning, for he repeated over and over the phrase 'Child of Bethlehem,' calling the word out, as it seemed to these country folk, like a sheep bleating, and his whole body seemed filled with love – to some it seemed as if the empty manger had indeed a living child in it; and from this preaching of Francis, to become one of the favourite legends of him, came a new sense and understanding of the Christmas story.

And so with many visits from passing friars, with characteristic scenes, where, finding some over-generous gift on their table, he would remind them by some gesture of Franciscan precept, he stayed till Easter was passed. From there, in June, he went to the chapter at Assisi, but seems very carefully to have abstained from any directing part in it, though a new mission that set out to England must have had his knowledge and his blessing. Then from there he went to Monte La Verna, the curious barren peak with its tuft of forest, to which Orlando of Chiusi had formerly invited him. It was a long steep journey, and Francis had to ask a peasant to let him ride on his mule. The man grew thirsty, but Francis showed him a spring in the dry hillside that no one knew of. This incident inspired one of the Assisi frescoes, one much admired by Vasari for its naturalness, and one that is very close to Giotto's manner. As they came further up the hill and rested, a flock of birds settled in the shrubs around them. Once more it was to a hermit life that Francis turned, and there went with him only a small band of the most faithful friends – Leo, Angelo Tancredi, Masseo, Rufino, Silvestro, Illuminato, Bonizzo – all tried friends who were very dear to him. Here, surrounded by the great cleft rocks, which reminded him of the cleaving of nature at the moment of Christ's death, Francis reached the climax of meditation. His soul was passing through strange experiences in the worn-out body, experiences which cannot be understood by others, nor rationalized in agreement with the limitation of our senses. Drawing apart even from such close friends, he abode in a shelter of branches on a rock ledge beyond a chasm, and Leo, who alone was near, was yet not allowed to cross the chasm unbidden by Francis. Strange doubts and torments were upon him:

he who strained nature in the service of his Lord suffered for it – suffered pains of body and mind, of dissolution; like ancient hermits, 'the devils worked anguish upon him'; and again Leo found him wrapt in close colloquy with the Divine. On the rock lip of La Verna Francis is a sick man, racked by hallucinations, disordered in mind and body, and knowing it; suffering torment of doubt and uncertainty, fighting through the weakness to which he had brought himself, to some greater certainty of faith. One night he bade Leo open, as himself had done so often, the Gospels at random, and three times Leo read to him the story of our Lord's Passion. Then, some days later, Francis called the little band together, and came down to them, and, as he asked them whether one should hide or reveal God's favours, they knew he was changed; and Francis told them of the Stigmata, how in a vision a seraph of the Lord had appeared to him, and how on his feet and hands and on his side he bore the marks of the Crucified. And brother Leo tended these bleeding wounds for him. A mystery was accomplished: this passionate spirit had achieved a strange material transformation; this imitation of Christ in the concentration of faith had achieved a miracle upon his own body, and in God's gift of it received a greatness of peace such as has rested upon very few of the elect. When he was dead the wounds were seen, blackened and swollen then – 'as nail-heads in the flesh,' Elias said – seen and testified to with careful authenticity, which leaves no doubt that at his death these wounds were beheld and believed in. How were they come by? There can be no serious doubt that he himself and the close friends believed in the existence of these wounds, and it is impossible to think that there was any conscious deception about them. How in that ecstacy on La Verna, when surely Francis had passed beyond normal perceptions, the signs formed themselves we cannot know. To his followers it was an event congruous with his life. 'The mind,' wrote Bonanventura, 'became apparent in the flesh.'

It was a failing man they brought down from the mountain, but a very joyful one. Before the departure, at Francis's bidding, Rufino had consecrated the rock where he had knelt to behold the seraphic vision, that rock which still is venerated today. And one other thing Francis had done: in the fulness of his heart, he had written down some of those praises of God, which he had always sought to sing and have his friars sing – simple words of praise, snatches, in the Latin of the breviary, from Psalms and Canticles, then, turning the page, he had written on it a blessing for brother Leo, signed it with the T, the Franciscan symbol, and given it him. And Leo confessed that he had read his heart aright, and that in the glorification of his master he had been sad for a new distance between them.

It was with brother Leo only, and with a peasant leading the ass on which he was mounted, that Francis now set out: they came by Monte Casale and Citta di Castello, and crowds gathered to see Francis, though the marks he bore were kept close secret; sometimes, weary in body and penetrating in spirit, he was dazed in ecstasy and heeded them not. By a night of wind and early sleet they came down from the hills to Assisi.

With the hurt of the wounds in his feet, Francis could hardly walk; his eyes failed him, and were bleared and painful; frequent sickness racked him from his disordered stomach; but he would not rest while any strength remained. That winter he rode on his ass throughout Umbria, sometimes with Elias, always, probably, with Leo, for he would not let others tend his wounds, though these now were healing somewhat. But by early summer the end seemed very near: he was nearly blind now, and even his energy failing. He wept now sometimes, from very weakness of the body, and in those moments remembered the troubles and disappointments of his Order. Elias wrote to Ugolino seeking advice. The papal court was at Rieti, driven there by a rising in Rome, and the cardinal strongly urged that Francis should come thither to receive treatment from the papal physicians; but, when he started out to go there, he was too weak to travel. They brought him into San Damiano, and there, for some six weeks, Clare nursed him, not only in body but in mind. When he was a little stronger, she made a wattle hut for him in their tiny garden, and he was grateful for this true Franciscanism. It is a dark little courtyard, the garden at Damiano: the rats ran across him in the night, and he could not sleep as he lay there ailing and unsightly. The fragrance of Francis's story is from within only. There, tending him, Clare must have learned of his secret wounds: in this month, she, too, had her reward. And it was lying there, his eyesight dimmed, that he wrote the Canticle of Brother Sun, lifting his heart in praise to God for that light which he himself was losing, for the sun, the moon and stars, fire and water, and all creatures:

> *Praise be to You, O Lord our God, with all of Your creation,*
> *Especially our good Sir Brother Sun,*
> *He which is day and lightens us thereby,*
> *And he is fair and radiant with great splendour*
> *And bears the Sign upon him of God Most High.*

It is a rough tongue, the early Italian that Francis used: the thoughts are those of the Psalmist, or the Song of the Three Children, but they have caught an intensity of feeling beyond all borrowing. Blind Milton, with his greater but embittered skill, could not invoke the light more nobly. With Francis it is all thanksgiving: the world is fair and kindly, and 'significant of God' (*de te, Altissimo, porta significatione*); God is not in nature in any pantheistic sense – God is in the Soul of Man, revealed to him most clearly in the sacrament which He ordained. But all nature bears His impress, and, to those rightly minded, the creature joyfully testifies to the Creator.

A little stronger, he set out to reach Rieti, and crowds gathered along the roadside to watch him; and the sick were brought to him to touch and heal. In the bishop's palace at Rieti he rested for a time. 'Borrow a lute,' he said, one day, to a brother, 'and bring comfort with some honest melody to Brother Body who is so full of pains.' But the brother urged that such playing of music would shock the devout. 'Let it be,' said Francis, 'it is better to be without good things than to scandalize others.' To the last they sought to conventionalize him, and now more than ever, when he was already hailed as a saint; but next morning Francis told them that angels had played to him. Then away from the crowds he went up to the hermitage at Fonte Colombo. There the doctors came to treat him.

He was told that they wished to cauterize his cheek, in an attempt to give relief to his eyes: for a moment the worn-out body shrank from the pain, and then, with a smile, the old spirit came back. 'Brother Fire,' he said, 'be courteous to me.' The agonizing treatment was in vain: needless pain for this ailing, incurable flesh. But at Christmas-time, once more he went out preaching in the villages. Every act now seemed to his earnest beholders a miracle; and the spirit shining through and moving the wasted body was miraculous. 'You think me a saint,' was all Francis said; 'I who all Advent have never fasted.' (For he had had to take nourishment he could best digest.) Perhaps there was some irony in his comment, and his thoughts turned to that earliest modification of his Rule and all that had been begun there.

In early spring he was in Siena, which was famed for its doctors; but one day there was a violent hæmorrhage; Francis himself thought it might be the end. Elias hurried to him. There was alarm in Assisi lest their saint should die outside their walls and they should be deprived of such a relic. An armed troop was sent to guard the dying man, for there was war once more with Perugia and the ways were dangerous. Never was Francis so welcomed as now,

PLATE XVI

JACOPA TENDS ST FRANCIS

When it was known that the Lady Jacopa was without, the friars hesitated because no woman was allowed to enter the Porziuncola. But Francis said 'This rule is not for this lady whom such faith and devotion has brought here from distant parts'. And she came in, and 'they received much consolation from seeing one another', and she kissed his feet, 'signed with the divine mark', and washed them with tears. (Actus Beati Francisci et Sociorum Ejus, C.XVIII)

15 — 25

almost a corpse and their own – a corpse that worked miracles, would give prestige, would bring pilgrims and profit: mixed, macabre motives, reminding us of the crudities from which grew Francis's high thoughts. So soldiers, his old fellow-prisoners, his old friends of feasting days, brought Francis by unfrequented detours, by Gubbio and Nocera, back to Assisi; and at one village they could not find food to buy, and Francis laughed at them and told them to go and beg for it, and the villagers gladly gave it them. They lodged him in the bishop's palace, for security, and waited for him to die. Leo, Angelo, Rufino, and Masseo were with him, and Pacifico, returned at this time from France. Sometimes these loyal friends could not hide how much they feared for the Order when he was gone. Francis himself had moments of despondency: 'Where are they who have taken away my brothers? Where are they who have stolen my family?' To Leo he dictated a message for the next chapter meeting, which he knew now he would not see, a message which he wished carefully preserved and kept on record. Clearly his mind was full of his defeat over the Rule, for this letter is an attempt to supplement it by those matters, so close to his heart, which the authorized Rule omitted: there is much about the sacrament, about preparation for receiving it, and about its administration – where there were several priests among a group of friars, he urged there should be but one celebration, 'the one for love being content to hear the other' – and about worship in general; that they shall 'attend not to the melody of the voice but the harmony of the mind'; and then, as ever, the personal note and the dominant pre-occupation are brought in. 'I confess that in many things I have offended gravely, especially since I have not kept the Rule, as I promised to God, nor said the office, as the Rule prescribes, either through negligence or by occasion of my infirmity or because I am ignorant and a fool.'

In the city, too, around him there were disputes: the bishop, still the same Guido, was quarrelling with the Podestà; Assisi seemed in strife as Francis had found it. Now, on his sick bed, he wrote a new verse of his Canticle:

Praised be You, O my Lord, for those that forgive for love of You
And bear infirmities and woes.
Blessed are those who will bear them in peace,
For by You, O most High, shall they be crowned.

And he sent this new verse to the Podestà, and the friars sang it about the streets, and, before this message of the dying saint, the quarrel ceased.

Some days later he added the final verse: a doctor from Arezzo came to visit him, and told him that he could not hope to live through the autumn. Angelo and Leo sang it for him:

Praised be You, O my Lord, for Sister Bodily Death
Whom no man living can escape.
Woe to those who die in mortal sin,
But blessed those who find themselves according to Your Will,
For them no second death shall harm.

The singing of St Francis and his companions shocked the Assisians a little; this was hardly how a saint died; Elias had to speak of it. Francis, too, was a little longer a-dying than had been expected. Finally they let him go to the peace and freedom of his beloved Porziuncola: he had promised to visit Clare if he could, but it was too long a round by San Damiano, and she herself was then sore sick, and could not come to him – it was only his body that was to be taken there. As they carried him down he turned to take his last look at Assisi and to bless the town.

And here, in the freshness of the woods, he found strength for his last work, the dictating of his Testament. It is not a thing that can be summarized or quoted from; looking back over his life he saw very clearly now what he had meant the order to be: he remembered how 'sweetness of soul' had come to him first in the case of lepers; of his restoring of Churches, his respect for priests, his faith in the sacra-ment; how the Lord had shown him the way of life and the pope confirmed it; of the early days of the Order, with how little they were content, labouring with their hands, begging alms; of their salutation, 'The Lord give you peace'; of his obedience, when the time came, to the minister-general and the guardian appointed by him. That was the past; he looked also to the future. 'I strictly command all the brethren that they shall not dare to ask any letter at the Roman Curia, through their own or other person's agency, neither for a church nor any other place, nor under pretext of preaching nor for protection in persecution.' If disputes arose, it was Ugolino who must settle them – 'the Lord Cardinal of Ostia is the protector and corrector of the whole brotherhood.' And this his Testament was no new Rule, but it should be read when the Rule was read. 'And I charge all my brothers, clerks and lay alike, by their obedience that they put no gloss upon the Rule nor upon these words. Saying, "So they are to be understood." But as the Lord gave me to speak and write the Rule and these words simply and purely, so simply and purely you shall understand them. . . . And I, Brother Francis, your little servant, inasmuch as I can, confirm unto you, within and without, this most holy blessing'.

It was over. Now in truth Francis was dying; but there was one last incident, as simple and moving as any that had gone before. With a sick man's fancy, he, the eater of fragments, thought of some marchpane cakes that Jacopa of Settesoli had often made for him – *frangipani* the Romans still call them, after the house she belonged to, and they were made doubtless from some family receipt. 'I believe,' said Francis, thinking of his friends and their coming grief, 'that the Lady Jacopa will hold it for a great consolation if you tell her of my state.' But before the letter had been sent, the brother who was acting as porter came hurrying to Francis: the Lady Jacopa and her sons were without, for, hearing the end was near, she had come, bringing all that was needful for tending him and for his burial. There was no woman allowed in the Porziuncola; Francis turned happily to them: 'Blessed be the Lord who has sent Brother Jacopa, for the Rule is not meant for her.' And she came in and watched by him till the end, bringing that reassurance which only women can give. (*Pls. XV, XVI*). To Clare also he sent a final message, bidding her not to mourn for him: and it was probably that message which later she put in her Rule:

'I, little Brother Francis, wish to follow the life and poverty of our most high Lord Jesus Christ and of His most holy Mother, and to persevere in it unto the end. And I beg you, my ladies, and I give you counsel, that you live always in this most holy life and poverty, and take much care of yourselves, lest, by the doctrine or advice of anyone, you ever depart from it.'

On Thursday, the first of October, he bade the brothers strip him and lay him on the ground, for he would die in true poverty: then he blessed them, beginning with Bernard of Quintavalle, his old friend and first disciple; next day he broke bread with them, simply and humbly, as his Master had done, and on the third, laid once more upon the ground, he died. Elias hastened to give to the world the news of the Stigmata: but others told how a great flight of larks had sung round St Mary of the Little Portion. Slowly they carried the corpse back up the hill to St George's Church, passing this time by San Damiano. And Clare came out to look once more upon him. And because of the sacred wounds all were joyful, but some of them, and Clare and Leo above all, knew that there was much striving to be done to preserve his heritage.

Within two years of his death, more speedily than in any known case of canonization, Francis was proclaimed a saint of the Church. Ugolino, now pope as Gregory IX, presided, and he and the cardinals, moved so much by their memories, could hardly complete their speeches for their so great weeping, till the people 'in their long expectation were wearied by the suspense'. With the Bull of Canonization came also the authorization to Elias to build a great church at Assisi, a noble if inappropriate setting for the precious relic of the corpse. Another two years passed, and Gregory, in the Bull, Quo Elongati commented on and expounded the Franciscan Rule. The Testament of Francis, he said, though undoubtedly 'drawn up with pious intention,' was not binding on them, for it had been issued without consultation with the ministers; since, also, the full imitation of the Gospel could hardly ever be 'literally observed,' the friars were only bound to those precepts particularly stated in the

Rule; for the rest, the use of property and payment of money through the mediation of some second party was authorized, and the visiting of the Poor Clares by any friars strictly prohibited.

On one of his visits to Assisi, Pope Gregory saw and talked with Clare at San Damiano. He was anxious that she should accept some endowment for her community, and assured her of his readiness to give the necessary dispensation. 'Holy Father,' she replied, 'never shall I wish to be dispensed from following Jesus Christ.' On her petition, also, the pope exempted her household of San Damiano, and Leo and others still came at times there to talk with her.

Sanctity is a perplexing subject because it passes our common understanding, and the cult of the saints has had curious practices, and sometimes a certain arbitrariness of selection, but the Christian thought of the world has found in this man a most especial holiness.

CHRONOLOGY

THERE is considerable controversy as to the exact chronology of the life of St Francis. The scope of this book does not permit of detailed argument, and in this, as in other uncertain points, I have had to state my conclusions without analysing the evidence that supports them. To those acquainted with the problems the debatable matter will be at once apparent; to the general reader I can only offer the assurance that my decisions have not been easily reached.

1181–2 Birth of Francis
1197 Death of the Emperor, Henry VI
1198 Accession of Pope Innocent III
Destruction of the Rocca of Assisi and setting up of consuls
1200 League of Assisian exiles with Perugia
1202 Battle of Collestrada: Francis taken prisoner
1203 Francis released from captivity: the commune of Assisi restores various privileges to the nobles
1205 Francis starts on an expedition to Apulia
1206 His conversion
1206–9 The restoration of churches
1209 First preaching: several disciples join him
1210 Innocent III approves his Rule
Assisi readmits the exiles
1211 The Porziuncola becomes the headquarters of the Order
1212 Francis receives Clare into the Order
1214–15 Francis visits Spain
1215 The Lateran Council. First meeting of Francis and Dominic
1216 Death of Innocent III and accession of Honorius III
Grant of indulgence to the Porziuncola

1217   Provincial organization. Francis plans to go to France, but is per-
        suaded against it by Ugolino
1219   New missions. Francis goes to Damietta and then to Syria. Issue of
        letters of authorization to the friars
1220   Return of Francis
        Peter Catani appointed minister-general
        Bull of Novitiate
1221   Death of Peter: Elias succeeds him
        The writing of the Rule
1223   Revision of the Rule
        29 November. It is approved by Honorius
        Christmas at Greccio
1224   *Aug.–Sept.* At La Verna. The Stigmata
1225   Ill in San Damiano: the Canticle of the Sun
1225–6 *Winter.* At Rieti
1226   *May.* Siena. Brought back to Assisi.
        3 October. Death of Francis
1227   Ugolino becomes pope as Gregory IX
1228   *16 July.* Canonization of St Francis
1230   *28 September.* Bull Quo Elongati

BIBLIOGRAPHY

SOURCES (in English)

The Writings of St Francis. Trans. P. Robinson. Philadelphia, 1906

Thomas of Celano, *Lives of St Francis*. Trans. A. G. Ferrers Howell. London, 1908

The Legend of the Three Companions. Trans. E. G. Salter. Temple Classics, 1905

Bonaventura, *Life of St Francis*. Trans. E. G. Salter. Temple Classics, 1904

Sacrum Commercium. Trans. Canon Rawnsley. Temple Classics, 1901

Life of St Clare, ascribed to Thomas of Celano. Trans. P. Robinson. Philadelphia, 1910

The Mirror of Perfection, Trans. L. Sherley-Price. London, 1959

L. Sherley-Price, *The Little Flowers of St Francis*. Penguin Classics, 1959

R. H. Moorman, *Sources for the Life of St Francis of Assisi*. Manchester, 1940 (Translations of the *Fioretti, The Mirror of Perfection* and Bonaventura's *Life* are published in one volume in Everyman's Library, No. 485, 1963.)

LATER WRITERS

P. Sabatier, *Vie de St François*. First pub. 1894; revised ed., 1931. Trans. L. S. Houghton, 1894

Father Cuthbert, *Life of St Francis*. London, 1912

L. Salvatorelli, *The Life of St Francis*. Trans. E. Sutton. London, 1928

St Francis of Assisi, 1226-1926. Essays in Commemoration. Ed. W. W. Seton. London, 1926

R. H. Moorman, *St Francis of Assisi,* London, 1963

I am greatly indebted to the *Nova Vita di San Francesco d'Assisi* by A. Fortini (Milan, 1926), which has not been translated into English.

INDEX